CEB A 1285
Modern Toys
19.95 Fine

MODERN TOYS

American Toys
1930-1980

MODERN TOYS

American Toys
1930-1980

Linda Baker

COLLECTOR BOOKS
A Division of Schroeder Publishing Co., Inc.

The current values in this book should be used as a guide. They are not intended to set prices, which vary from one section of the country to another. Auction prices as well as dealer prices vary greatly and are affected by condition as well as demand. Neither the Author nor the Publisher assumes responsibility for any losses that might be incurred as a result of consulting this guide.

For my children, Molly and Sam

A Note To The New Collector

Collecting modern toys is fun. In most cases, it is a far less costly treasure hunt than seeking the true antiques, as well as more easily done. The gratification of coming upon that long-searched-for toy is wonderful, but the thrill of the hunt is what appeals to most of us. With rare exception, you will find "toy people" an agreeable lot and you may form many new friendships.

The Toys In This Book

Most of the toys pictured here are from my own collection. If a toy belongs to someone else or the photograph was taken by someone else, credit is given beneath the photo. I want to thank the "toy people" from all over the country who have sold me toys, sent their toys to me to photograph and return, or who have sent photos of their own toys for my use. They are as generous and helpful a group as could be found anywhere. Special thanks to a special lady, Mary E. McCaughey, for her help in getting this book in shape for the printers; and thanks to my friend, Sharon Vantuyl, for supplying several playset pieces to complete my sets for the photos.

Table of Contents

THE AIRO-PLAK CORPORATION

1 - JUNIOR SET CARPET SWEEPER - Painted metal body is nailed to painted wooden end pieces. Wooden wheels are attached with screws, as is the painted metal handle bracket. Wooden handle with wooden end knob is attached to metal bracket with brass fitting. Picture appears to be an applied decal. Natural bristle brush picks up dirt. $9^3/_8$" x $7^1/_4$" x 23" overall height. c. late 1940s.

Gifts that really thrill any little child's heart — lovable toy animals that soothe a toddler's tumbles and games that keep busy little bodies quiet while they spur on active brains!
Games and toys that are sturdily built to stand up under a lot of rough and tumble. Toys that are gay in waterproof coloring and of irresistible appeal.

A nice Quacky Duck or a Questioning Giraffe

There is Mrs. Quack Duck, all dressed up in latest fashion, hat with a gay nosegay — or her friend husband in manly attire. Smarty Dog — a pugnacious pup. Humpty Hump the Camel or Billy, the Goat — any one or all of All Fair animals will delight any small person on your list. Each animal attractively packaged in colorful lithographed box for $1.00. For little tots from 2 to 6.

Combination Tennis and Baseball Game

Combines two of best loved sports in a lively and exciting game for $1.00. This is positively biggest game value you can buy anywhere! For boys and girls from 5 to 10.

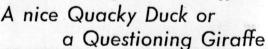

"Our Gang"—a la Hal Roach

The lovable, troublesome gang that children follow in the movies — now a game exclusive with All Fair. Entirely new principle of play. $1.00. For boys and girls from 4 to 9.

ALL-FAIR TOY COMPANY

2X - Herman G. Fisher, co-founder of the Fisher-Price Toy Co., worked for this Churchville, N.Y., company before starting his own. Ad from 1930 *Child Life* magazine. Courtesy of Bianca Hoekzema.

Play "Store" with Stop and Shop

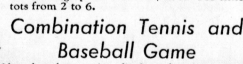

A game that always goes over big. Plenty of action and it teaches children how to buy. 50c. For girls and boys from 4 to 10.
Each and every All Fair game and toy is a sure way to make Christmas a success with the children! If you can't find the All Fair toy or game you want, send money and coupon below to All Fair, Inc.,   5 Toy Street, Churchville, N.Y.

ALL-FAIR, Inc.
5 Toy Street
Churchville, N. Y.

Please send me, postpaid

☐ ....
☐ ....
☐ ....
☐ ....

Name.............................. Street or R.F.D.
City.............................. State.
If not satisfactory you are to return the money.

AMERICAN METAL SPECIALTIES CORP.

3 - AMSCO KIDD-E SHU-SHINE BANK - 8½" L. x 6" W. x 8" H. Painted metal shoeshine box has red plastic shoulder carrying strap and picture decals on side and end. Coins are inserted into a slot in the end. Originally came with shoe polish, brushes, and cloth. c. 1952.

4 - AMSCO DOLL-E-DISH TIME - Card is 11½" x 6". Dish washing accessories include a small box of Brillo pads, a DuPont sponge, Rymplecloth polishing fabric, a bottle brush and a brittle plastic sink strainer. c. 1955. Price in 1955 - 29¢.

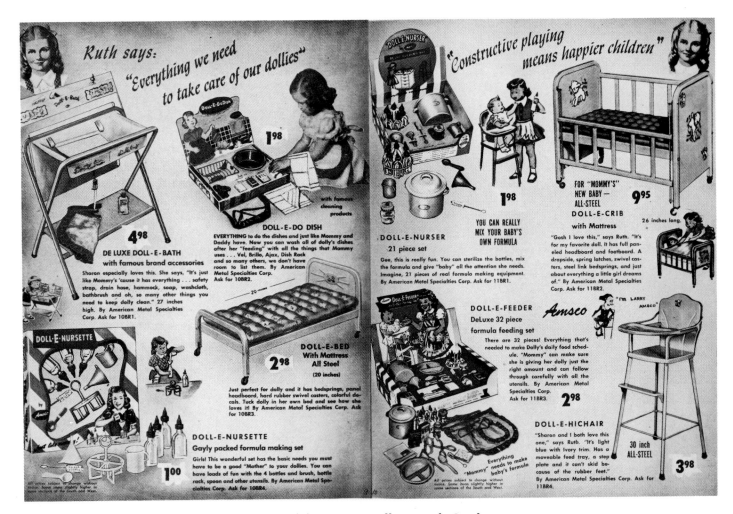

5X - Ad from 1952 *Billy & Ruth Catalog.*

ANIMAKERS

6 - ANIMAKERS - Box is 6¾" x 10¼". Colored wooden shapes fit together to make various animals. c. 1945.

ARCHER PLASTICS "CHILD GUIDANCE TOYS-- WHERE CHILDHOOD DREAMS COME TRUE"

7 - ED-U-PHONE - 6" x 6" x 4" H. Brittle plastic take-apart phone has eight multi-colored pieces to fit together. c. 1953. Original price in 1953 - $1.49.

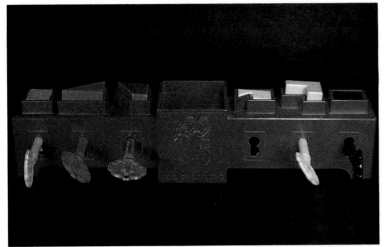

8A - KEYS OF LEARNING - 16¼″ L. x 3¾″ H. Heavy red plastic base holds colored plastic shapes which can be popped up by inserting the same color plastic key into the hole below it and turning. The shapes can be fitted into the center square, puzzle fashion. (White key not shown.) Each key and keyhole shape is unique. c. 1953. Original price in 1953 - $2.98.

8B - Close up of Keys of Learning.

"IT'S AN ARROW TOY-AIMED AT THE HEARTS OF CHILDREN"

9 - TERRIER - 9″ L. x 6½″ W. x 10″ H. Molded vinyl terrier-type dog has a turning head and eyes that open and close. Squeaker. c. 1960.

10 - BOWSER WOWSER - 20″ L. x 5½″ W. x 10¼″ H. Vinyl spaniel dog has turning head, eyes that open and close and a squeaker. Fake fur fabric ears are lined with red satin-like material. c. 1962.

11 - LI'l BEEP BUS - 11″ L. x 6½″ H. One piece molded vinyl bus "beeps" when squeezed. It rolls along on red plastic "balloon" wheels mounted off-center. Red pull string. c. 1965. Price in 1965 - $2.49.

12 - KITTY - 5¼″ L. x 3½″ W. x 5¾″ H. Molded vinyl cat has turning head and squeaker. c. 1960.

ARTWOOD TOY MFG. CO.

13 - SOLDIER TEN PINS - Soldiers: 7½″ H. Set of 10 painted wooden soldiers and three painted balls. Hats are a separate piece.

B.F. JAY

14 - B. F. JAY - "UNCLE BEN JAY'S JUMBLE JUNGLE" - Set consists of four books. One book shows animal heads, one upper body, one lower body and one legs. A poem accompanies each picture. Bizarre animals and nonsensical poems are formed by combining pages from each book. c. 1942.

BACHMAN BROS. PLASTICVILLE, U.S.A.

15 - Heavy brittle plastic components fit together with dovetailed edges to make buildings. Many accessory pieces came with the sets. The photo shows pieces from a barn made in the early 1950s on the left and the same pieces from a currently available barn. The biggest change has been in the thickness of the plastic. These sets were scaled to go with model trains.

11

Plasticville, U.S.A.

The Town That GROWS and GROWS

MAKES YOUR TRAIN SET MORE COMPLETE

5.00 RURAL UNIT

This depicts real country living and is what you need for the outskirts of your little village. 1 barn, 1 Cape Cod house, 1 log cabin, 2 boxes of fence, 1 yard pump, 1 bridge and pond, 1 outhouse, 1 bag of shrubs, 2 spruce trees, 2 maple trees, 6 cows, 2 horses, 4 pigs, 4 sheep. You can almost smell the "new mown" hay. By Bachmann Bros. Ask for 27BR1.

2.50 BARN AND ANIMAL UNIT

by BACHMAN BROS.

Now — a real farm for your train outfit! It's complete with 1 barn, 2 boxes white fence, 1 maple tree, 4 pigs, 4 sheep, 3 painted cows, 4 solid colored cows, 2 horses solid colors, 1 painted horse. Everyone will love this. By Bachmann Bros. Ask for 27BR2.

2.50 TRAIN ACCESSORIES UNIT

"Say Ruth, this will really dress up our train station," says Billy. "Look what it has — 1 railroad station, 1 freight station, 2 railroad crossing gates, 4 telephone poles, 2 billboards, 2 street lamps, 1 evergreen tree and 2 benches. Don't they look real?" By Bachmann Bros. Ask for 27BR3.

SHOPPING UNIT 5.00

Give part of your set-up that "city look." Here's 1 police station, 1 super market, 1 gas station, 1 fire house, 1 diner, 2 boulevard lights, 2 street signs, 1 each: fire hydrant, fire alarm box, mail box, and 2 traffic lights. Perfect for the modern touch. By Bachmann Bros. Ask for 27BR4.

All prices subject to change without notice. Some items slightly higher in some sections of the South and West.

16X - Plasticville from 1952 *Billy and Ruth Catalog.*

J. CHEIN AND CO.

17 - SEE-SAW SAND TOY - 7″ H. Metal litho sand toy. Sand running through funnel creates see-saw action. c. 1935. Courtesy of Margaret Mandel. Photo by Margot Mandel.

18 - DOLLY'S WASHER - 7¾″ H. x 5″ Dia. Metal litho washing machine has inside agitator that moves up and down when handle is turned. c. 1930.

19 - SANDPAIL - 4¾″ square at top, 3³/₈″ square at bottom, 6″ T., 9″ including handle. Metal litho sand pail has price sticker on side which reads: "F. W. Woolworth Co., 29¢."

20 - SAND SHIP AND SCOOP - 8½″ L. x 3½″ W. x 3½″ H. Metal litho ship has wheels for pulling as well as a handle for carrying. (Original shovel had wooden dowel handle.)

21 - SANDPAIL AND SHOVEL - 4½″ H. bucket. Square metal litho pail and matching shovel. *Courtesy of and photo by Kathryn Fain.*

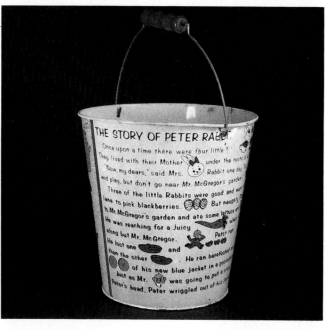

22 SANDPAIL - 8″ H. x 8″ Dia. Metal litho bucket with wire bail, wooden handle, and word-and-picture rendition of "Peter Rabbit" around the outside.

23 - WIND-UP DUCK - 3¾″ H. Metal litho duck has wind-up tail. He wobbles back and forth on separate feet. *Courtesy of and photo by Kathryn Fain.*

24 - MARK I SPEEDBOAT - 8½″ L. Two color variations of the same wind-up, propeller-driven metal litho boat.

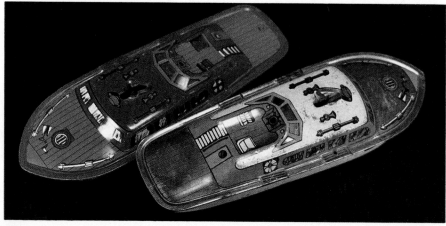

25 - ROLLER COASTER - 19½″ L. x 8¼″ W. x 10¼″ H. Metal litho roller coaster has wind-up "motor" which brings train up to the top of the track. "Cog chain" is a piece of elastic with metal prongs clamped to it. c. 1970.

26 - SPIRAL TOP - 6½″ Dia. Metal litho top has yellow plastic knob. Disney character motif. 1970s.

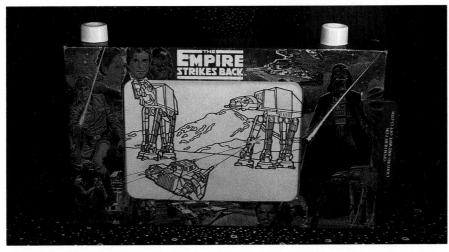

CRAFT MASTER

27 - CRAFT MASTER - Color 'n Clean Machine. 14″ x 9¼″ x 2″. Cardboard box contains 50″ continuous roll of "Empire" action scenes to color, four crayons and a wipe-off cloth. c. 1980.

15

CREATIVE PLAYTHINGS

28 - HAND PUPPET FAMILY - Baby. 9″ H. Painted flexible rubber hand puppet is part of a five-piece family, which sold for $9.50 in 1969 and came as either a white or a black family. Marked 1955.

29 - ALARM CLOCK - 6″ H. x 4″ W. Real working wind-up alarm clock has clear plastic face to show gears moving. Red metal back, chrome bells, brass handle, and feet.

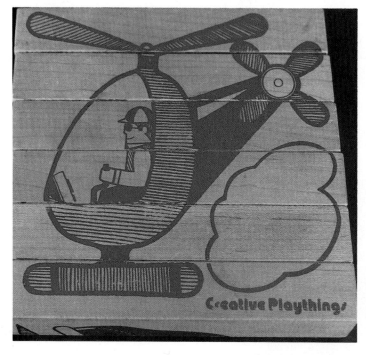

30A and 30B - BLOCK PUZZLE - Six rectangular wooden blocks can be laid side by side to make four different pictures.

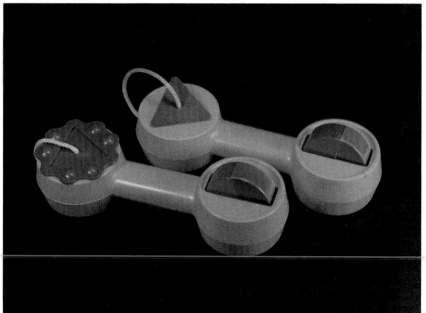

31 - ACTIVITY TOY - 7″ L. Yellow plastic dumbbell-shaped infant toy. One end has mirror on one side and a spinning cylinder on the other. The opposite end has a "phone" dial on one side and a triangular shape to fit into a corresponding depression on the other. Two versions of the same toy are pictured.

32 - RIDE-ON-TOY - Red fiberboard seat, wooden frame and blue plastic "balloon" wheels. Front wheels turn.

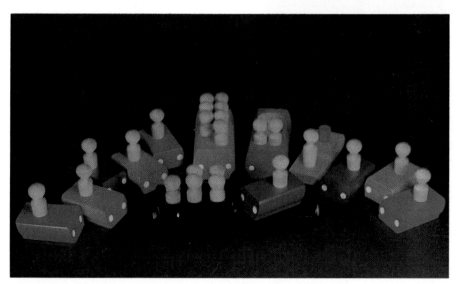

33 - BLOCKOMOBILES - Cars are 2¼″ L. Small solid wood block vehicle set includes one boat, one bus, one train, two trucks, ten cars, three trees, and 30 peg people. Comes in white plastic tub with red and blue printing.

34- CHANGING FACES - 7½″ H. Molded plastic manipulative infant toy. Three horizontally revolving cylinders make many facial creations possible.

35 - WOODEN MANIPULATIVE TOYS - Infant toys roll, push, pull and clatter.

36 - AMERICAN INDIAN PEOPLE AND PLACES - 23-piece playset includes: base piece, hill, tepee and top, campfire, leather drying rack, meat drying rack, three figures, two horses and one horse blanket, travois, buffalo and coyote. Two other sets in this group were Eskimos and South American Indians. c. 1975.

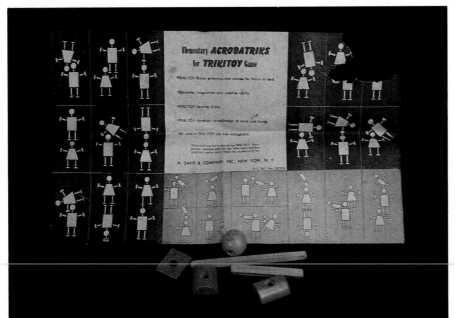

H. DAVIS & CO.

37 - H. DAVIS & CO. TRIKITOY - These few wooden pieces from a larger set were found with the instruction sheet. The figures created would balance in various positions together or separately. c. 1940.

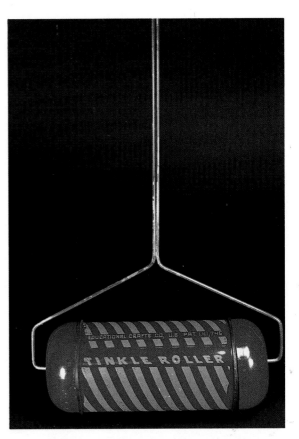

EDUCATIONAL CRAFT CO.

39 - EDUCATIONAL CRAFT COMPANY "TINKLE ROLLER" - Roller 7″ x 2½″ Dia.; handle 21½″ L.; overall 26″ L. Painted metal roller is a cylinder with separate semi-spherical ends that push on. Removable black rubber "bands" provide traction. Bent wire handle is painted blue. The "tinkle" in this toy is provided by five finish nails inside roller. Late 1940s.

DURHAM

38 - DURHAM "PERFORMING CLOWN" - Plunger-activated spring mechanism makes clown turn side to side and beat drum. Clown head, hands and feet and drum heads are plastic; drum base is cardboard; and clown body is cloth and wire. c. 1975.

EMENEE

40 - EMENEE "GOLDEN PIANO ACCORDIAN" - 12" H., extends to nearly 24". Deluxe model play accordian has plastic body, 18 keys and 52 tuned reeds. Came in cardboard case with song book and harness strap. c. 1957. Price in 1957 - $7.24.

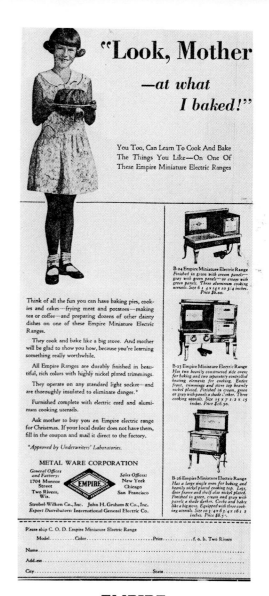

EMPIRE

41X - EMPIRE - Ad from December 1930 *Child Life* magazine. Courtesy of Bianca Hoekzema.

FAIRLINE PLASTICS

42 - FAIRLINE PLASTICS "RINGING PHONE" - Brittle plastic phone has wind-up mechanism on the right side. When red button on the front is pushed, phone rings. c. 1950.

43 - EMPIRE ELECTRIC STOVE - 16" H. Courtesy of Jean Couch. Photo by Jerry Couch.

FISHER-PRICE TOYS

In 1930, Irving L. Price had recently retired from his position with the F. W. Woolworth Company and was serving as Mayor of East Aurora, N. Y. He was looking for new business ventures for the village and approached Herman G. Fisher, who at that time was working for the Alderman-Fairchild Toy Company in Churchville, N.Y. Helen M. Schelle was a former operator of the Penny Walker Toy Shop at Binghamton, N.Y. Together, these three people formed a company which was to become one of the best known manufacturers of toys in this country. Margaret Evans Price, wife of the founder and illustrator for children's books, took a large part in the designing of the first 16 toys made by the company. Herman Fisher resigned as president in 1966 and was succeeded by Henry H. Coords. Then, in 1969, Fisher-Price Toys was acquired by the Quaker Oats Company.

REGARDING FISHER-PRICE TOYS
SHOWN IN THIS BOOK

Since Fisher-Price conveniently and obviously numbers, as well as names their toys, the toys are listed here by number. When a toy bearing a certain number has been out of production for three or four years, that number is re-assigned to a new toy. In the instance of duplicate numbers, the oldest toy will be shown first. An overwhelming majority of Fisher-Price Toys are made of paper lithographs applied over a wooden base. To avoid tedious repetition in description, please assume that the toy is so constructed unless otherwise noted. Two helpful guides in the preliminary dating of any of these toys are these: the black and white rectangular logo appears on all toys prior to 1962; and anything made with ANY plastic part was made after 1949. No actual photos of the original 16 toys are shown here; but the 1931 catalog, the first one put out by the company, is reproduced for your enjoyment and enlightenment.

44X-52X - Nine pages from the *Fisher-Price 1931 Catalog of Action Wood Toys,* showing the original 16 toys offered by this company. Copyright 1931 Fisher-Price, Inc.; reprinted with permission.

FISHER-PRICE TOYS, INC. EAST AURORA, .N. Y.

WHEELUM
PULL TOYS

Styled by
Margaret Evans Price

quack! quack!

quack! quack!

Pat. applied for

Pat. applied for

101—GRANNY DOODLE—101

GRANNY DOODLE — an experienced dame but young for her years —knows just how children play. She follows them—neck going up and down with waddling motion, bill opening and closing as she quacks "Play! Play!" The youthful tilt of her *felt* bonnet makes her a gay old bird. Concealed squawker. Four-color photo-lithography. Easy seller at $1.

Packing: Individual gayly colored corrugated box; 1 dozen to shipping container.
Size of toy: 6½" long x 10¾" high x 4" wide.
Shipping weight per dozen: 15 lbs.

100—DOCTOR DOODLE—100

DOCTOR DOODLE — an important duck—struts along in his waddling way, neck rising and falling, bill opening and closing, quack-quacking all the time. His self-importance, emphasized by the bright four-color photo-lithography, wins the youngsters every time. Just notice the plug hat. Concealed squawker ► Big value for your customer's $1.00.

Packing: Individual gayly colored corrugated box; 1 dozen to shipping container.
Size of toy: 7" long x 11½" high x 4" wide.
Shipping weight per dozen: 15 lbs.

ACTION WOOD TOYS OF STRONG CONSTRUCTION

ACTION WOOD TOYS WITH INGENUITY

WHEELUM
PULL TOYS

Styled by
Margaret Evans Price

woof! woof! woof!

Pat. Pending

Pat. applied for

103—BARKY PUPPY—103

BARKY PUPPY is a noisy, frisky, little fellow. He crouches on his forelegs, tilts up his head and barks mock protest as his child-master pulls him along. A lovable puppy body, an expression full of play, a loud bark and fine four-color photo-lithography make him irresistible. Concealed barker ► Fast moving at $1.00

Packing: Individual gayly colored corrugated box; 1 dozen to shipping container.
Size of toy: 10½" long x 10" high x 4" wide.
Shipping weight per dozen: 19½ lbs.

104—LOOKEE MONK—104

LOOKEE MONK, full of pep and curiosity, wants to see everything. His head turns from side to side to look at every bit of child life about him as he pedals along with busy legs racing. Kiddies love this whimsical expression, appealingly done in four-color photo-lithography and mounted on wood ► Sells itself at $1.00

Packing: Individual gayly colored corrugated box; 1 dozen to shipping container.
Size of toy: 9" long x 10¾" high x 4" wide.
Shipping weight per dozen: 19½ lbs.

FISHER-PRICE TOYS, INC. EAST AURORA, N. Y.

WALKY-BALKY

(TRADE-MARK)

The ONLY motor-
they WALK FOR
but at unfo

Styled by
Margaret Evans Price

Sensational New Toy That You Need

RETAILERS know that every industry needs a sensational new item to stimulate buying all along the line. On these pages you have discovered the Walky-Balky-Backups, answering this demand for the toy industry. Build your toy campaign on the willing Walky-Balky-Backup. He has the power to carry you thru.

Startling New Action

Propelled by faultless motor, these toys walk forward and back-up, not automatically like a shuttle train, but unpredictably. Each toy has a personality of its own, with individual differences in character, just like so many live animals. An absolutely different action principle.

FISHER PRICE TOYS
CREATED AT EAST AURORA N.Y.

Pat. Pending

350—GO 'n' BACK MULE—350

As a toy, Go 'n' Back Mule has the stubbornness and lovable whimsicality of the whole mule species. Each toy with the different mulish individuality and the "you can't tell what he'll do" character of a live mule. More volume and more plus value at $1.50 than in toys selling at twice that.

As a game, there's more real sport in matching these animals against each other than in any horse-race game made. Good for straight-away up to fifty feet and you can't pick the winner till he crosses the line —because there's no telling when Walky-Balky-Backup toys will stop and back up.

Packing: Individual gayly colored corrugated box; 1 dozen to shipping container.
Size of toy: 9" long x 10" high x 3½" wide. Bright four-color photo-lithography.
Shipping weight per dozen: 17½ lbs.

FISHER - PRICE TOYS, INC. EAST AURORA, N. Y.

BACKUP TOYS

(Pat. Pendin)

...anical wood toys that walk—AND
...nd BACK-UP, not automatically,
..., like a live conscious animal

Volume Makes Low Price Possible

IT seems ambitious to bring out a sensational toy worth $2.50 and price it to sell in the $1.50 class. As toy makers we are making *the best toy possible,* regardless of price. As business men we are taking a tip from Ford and lowering the figure to the minimum, confident of volume production.

Long Lasting Motor

It took six months' experimentation to perfect the motor. Each working part double thick and rigidly encased to make a long-distance long-duty motor. An expert motor manufacturer, who produced the outstanding strong motor of the last two years, is making these motors for us.

Pat. Pending

GO 'n' BACK BRUNO - 355

BRUNO with his brand new action takes youngsters by storm. Wind him up, start him off—and immediately he thinks and acts for himself. Forward and back, there's no telling when he'll change. With a strong motor working his legs, Bruno has good lasting power.

Packing: Individual gayly colored corrugated box; 1 dozen to shipping container.
Size of toy: 9" x 6" high x 3½" wide. Bright four-color photo-lithography.
Shipping weight per dozen: 17½ lbs.

Pat. Pending

GO 'n' BACK JUMBO - 360

PLODDING determined gait, body swaying from side to side, trunk swinging in rhythm—Jumbo has them all—and more! He surprises and fascinates —he walks forward, stops whenever he wants to and backs up. His well made motor gives him elephantine strength.

Packing: Individual gayly colored corrugated box; 1 dozen to shipping container.
Size of toy: 9" long x 6¾" high x 3½" wide. Bright four-color photo-lithography.
Shipping weight per dozen: 19 lbs.

FISHER PRICE TOYS
CREATED AT EAST AURORA N.Y.

WHEN WE SAY SENSATION—WE MEAN JUST THA

FISHER-PRICE TOYS, INC. EAST AURORA, N. Y.

WOODSY-WEE TOYS
TRADE MARK

Styled by Margaret Evans Price   Pat. applied for

WOODSY-WEE CIRCUS
TRADE MARK

No. 201

Lion - Camel - Giraffe - Elephant
Baby Elephant - Dog - Pony - Bear
Monkey - Clown - Cart

NINE favorite animals, a clown and a cart (total eleven items) just the right size to climb into a youngster's heart—that's the Woodsy-Wee Circus. Line them up, hook them together and the grandest Circus Parade will roll along on easy turning bead wheels. Or just connect Pony and Cart—or hunt Lion and Elephant in the nursery jungle. Actual tests with children in the home have proved the unequalled intrinsic play value of Woodsy-Wee Toys. Best $1.25 value for your customer.

Giraffe 5½" high, Monkey 2¼" high, others in proportion. Designs in four-color photo-lithography, mounted on ⅜" wood. Colored bead wheels ⅝" in diameter. Each toy has two connecting hooks with points carefully turned out of baby's reach.

Packing: One-quarter dozen in paper package; one dozen in shipping container.
Size: Four-color photo-lithographed box 16" long x 12" wide x 1¾" deep.
Shipping weight per dozen: 23 lbs.
Parts: 9 wood animals, wood cart, wood clown.

ACTION WOOD TOYS—GOOD VALUE FOR THE MONEY

ACTION WOOD TOYS WITH INTRINSIC PLAY VALUE

WOODSY-WEE TOYS
TRADE MARK

Pat. applied for

WOODSY-WEE ZOO
TRADE MARK

No. 205

Elephant - Lion - Camel - Bear - Giraffe

WOODSY-WEE ZOO has five wild animals. The animals that little brother thrills to capture and train. He'll even clutch Baby Bear in his chubby fist as he slips off to the Land of Nod. Cuteness, lovableness and playfulness have replaced fierceness in the Woodsy-Wee Zoo. Much more than 65c worth of fun.

Lithographed tray, ⅝" deep, holds animals in marked died-out locations. Colored bead wheels ⅝" in diameter. Each toy has two connecting hooks with points carefully turned out of baby's reach.

Packing: One-half dozen in paper package; two dozen in shipping container.
Size: Four-color photo-lithographed box 10½" long x 9" wide x 1¾" deep.
Shipping weight per dozen: 12 lbs.
Parts: 5 wood animals.

Styled by Margaret Evans Price

Pat. applied for

WOODSY-WEE PETS
TRADE MARK

No. 207

Cow - Pig - Goat - Cart - Donkey

A CART and four farm pets not in either of the other two sets. The pets that baby first sees in picture books and learns to love. Toys to stimulate the child's imagination by happy play hours with whimsical, true-to-life animals. Like the Circus and Zoo—superlative value for the money. Great seller at 65c.

Lithographed tray ⅝" deep, holds animals in marked died-out locations. Colored bead wheels ⅝" in diameter. Each toy has two connecting hooks with points carefully turned out of baby's reach.

Packing: One-half dozen in paper package; two dozen in shipping container.
Size: Four-color photo-lithographed box 10½" long x 9" wide x 1¾" deep.
Shipping weight per dozen: 12 lbs.
Parts: 4 wood animals and wood cart.

FISHER-PRICE TOYS, INC. EAST AURORA, N. Y.

FISHER-PRICE TOYS, INC. EAST AURORA, N. Y.

POP-UP KRITTERS

(Patented October 5, 1926—No. 1,601,983)

POP-UP KRITTER action and construction is patented and exclusive with Fisher-Price Toys.

Invalid youngsters in bed, healthy rascals on the floor, restless kiddies on long train or auto trips find heaps of fun in the always new action of Pop-Up Kritters. Grown-ups, too, enjoy their ingenuity. They are ideal bridge prizes or novel favors.

Bead and string construction allow Pop-Up Kritters to spring up, squirm and crumple with a pull on the string. Always different attitudes, always different actions.

DIZZY DINO
No. 407

I'm Dizzy Dino, if you please,
Full of life from nose to knees.
Just buy me quick
And learn the trick—
I'm made for fun, the world agrees.

Standards: 7½" high, 13½" nose to tail. Lacquer finish. A great animal in the $1 class.
Packing: Individual varnished four-color lithographed box; 3 dozen to shipping container.
Size: Box 13¾" x 4⅝" x 1¾".
Shipping weight per dozen: 7 lbs.

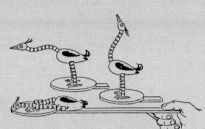

Showing typical positions of POP-UP KRITTER. They always have a surprise for you.

STOOPY STORKY
No. 410

I'm Stoopy Storky (wise old bird),
Dignified yet most absurd.
I twist and turn
From stem to stern,
The newest toy you've seen or heard.

Standards: 7½" high. Lacquer finish. Something totally new for 75c.
Packing: Individual varnished four-color lithographed box; 3 dozen to shipping container.
Size: Box 13¾" x 4⅝" x 1¾".
Shipping weight per dozen: 6 lbs.

ACTION WOOD TOYS WITH INGENUITY

VOLUME GETTERS FROM FEBRUARY TO DECEMBER

POP-UP KRITTERS

(Patented Oct 5, 1926—No 1,601,98)

A FINGER'S pressure on the rings and up go the Pop-Up Kritters. See-saw the rings—Tailspin Tabby's tail becomes alive—it twitches from top to bottom, with the true-to-life action of a real cat's tail.

Relax the fingers — forelegs bend, tail droops, head sways—down crumples Mr. Pop-Up Kritter. Each time in a different position. There's no telling beforehand what he'll do. Always ready to pop up again and fidget into new positions with new twists and squirms.

LOFTY LIZZY
No. 405

I'm Lofty Lizzy to my friends—
I'm full of funny falls and bends.
Just work my string
A simple thing,
The fun begins and never ends.

Standards: 7" high. Lacquer finish. Sells fast at 75c.
Packing: Individual varnished four-color lithographed box; 3 dozen to shipping container.
Size: Box 13¾" x 4⅝" x 1¾".
Shipping weight per dozen: 6 lbs.

For different action, just tighten or relax finger. There's always surprise in a POP-UP KRITTER.

TAILSPIN TABBY
No. 400

Tailspin Tabby is my name—
Action is my claim to fame.
Who can resist
My tail to twist
To pass me up would be a shame.

Standards: 4½" high. Tail 4" long. Lacquer finish. Big play value for $1.
Packing: Individual varnished four-color lithographed box; 3 dozen to shipping container.
Size: Box 13¾" x 4⅝" x 1¾".
Shipping weight per dozen: 7 lbs.

FISHER-PRICE TOYS, INC. EAST AURORA, N. Y.

53 - #7 DOGGY RACER - 10¼″ x 4½″ H. Black felt arms. 1942-45.

54 - #7 LOOKY FIRE TRUCK - 12″ x 4½″ x 5″ H. Plastic hats, metal bell. Hammer strikes bell, eyes roll up and down, two firemen in back spin. 1950-54.

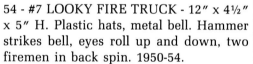

55 - #8 BOUNCY RACER - 9¾″ x 6⁵/₈″ x 4″ H. Plastic balloon wheels, windshield, helmet, arms and steering wheel. 1960-70. Price in 1963 - $1.59.

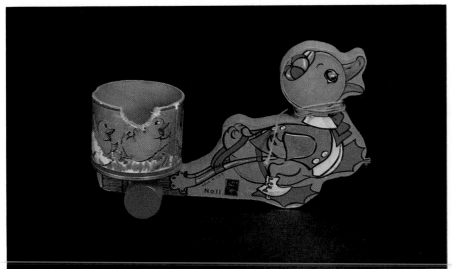

56 - #11 DUCKY CART - 8¼″ L. x 5″ H. Cylinder: 2¾″ Dia. Cardboard cylinder has a metal bottom. (The "bite" out of the edge of the cylinder was nibbled out by a mouse who either liked the flavor of the glue used or needed just a bit more nesting material! An otherwise mint toy from an old store.) 1940-42.

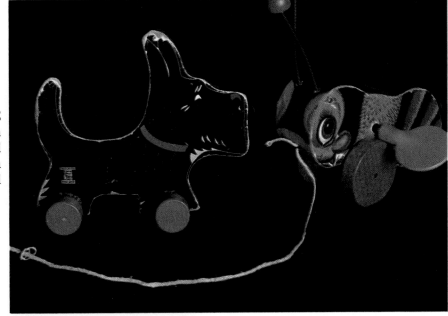

57 - #20 ANIMAL CUTOUT SCOTTIE DOG - 6″ L. This was part of a set which included the Scottie, pony, duck and elephant. Courtesy of Sandy Witherspoon and Barbara B. Davis. Photo by Howard Davis. 1942-43; 1946-49.

58 - #100 MUSICAL SWEEPER - Base: 8½″ x 7″ x 3″ H. Metal litho top, wooden ends and wheels. Wooden handle. 1950-1952.

59 - #104 ANIMAL SCRAMBLE GAME - 8¼" x 7¼" x 7½" H. All plastic toy with paper lithos. 1971-72.

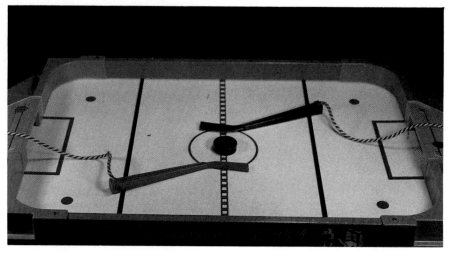

60 - #109 HOCKEY GAME - 30½" L. x 16½" W. x 2" H. Hockey "field" is painted Masonite, end pieces are plastic. Plastic hockey sticks are fastened to each end by red and white cord. Two plastic pucks, one red and one blue. Bell rings when goal is scored. 1974-76.

61 - #111 MUSIC BOX MERRY-GO-ROUND - 11" x 8¾" base. Mostly plastic toy on Masonite base. Boy figure in ball cap appears to turn the crank to "The Skater's Waltz." 1972-77.

62 - #112 CHANGEABLE PICTURE DISC CAMERA - 5″ x 4¼″ x 3″. All plastic camera has paper litho design on flash cube and on back. Includes color wheel and four picture discs. Plastic wrist strap. 1968-70.

63 - #118 TUMBLE TOWER - 3″ x 3″ x 10½″ H. Clear plastic rectangular box with five compartments and built-in sand timer. Ten white marbles must be manipulated from level to level before sand runs out. 1972-75.

64 - #120 CACKLING HEN - 10″ H. x 6½″ L. Box construction conceals inner clucking mechanism. Vinyl comb and tail feathers. 1958-66.

65 - #131 HAPPY HOPPERS - Mostly plastic push toy has wooden handle with plastic end knob. 1969-76.

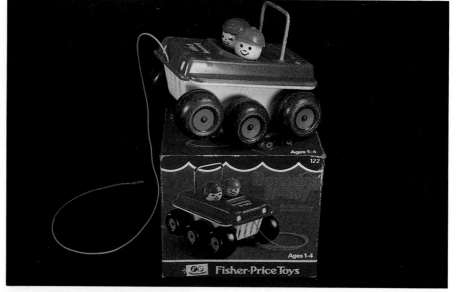

66 - #122 BOUNCING BUGGY - 6½″ x 4¾″ x 5¾″ H. All plastic with metal roll bar. 1973-79.

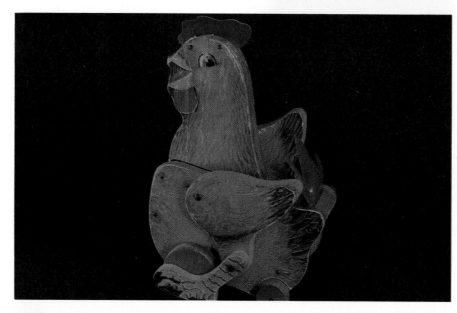

67 - #123 CACKLING HEN - 10″ H. x 6½″ L. Box construction conceals inner cackling mechanism. Vinyl comb and tail feathers. 1966-68.

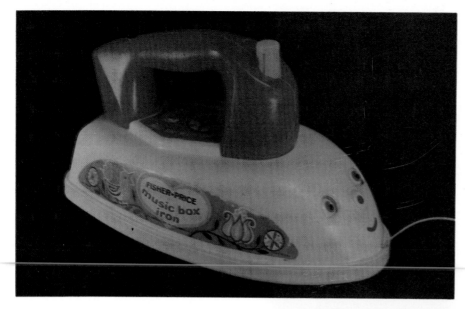

68 - #125 MUSIC BOX IRON - 8″ L. x 4″ H. Plastic with paper lithos. Eyes roll. Music box plays when iron is pushed back and forth. 1966-68.

69 - #130 WOBBLES - 14″ x 8½″ x 9″ H. Hollow black vinyl ears, green vinyl collar and yellow balloon wheels. (Red vinyl tongue missing.) Spring tail. 1964-67.

70 - #131 TOY WAGON - 17″ x 4⁷/₈″ x 7¼″ H. This example is a beautiful toy, absolutely M.I.B. The team of horses rocks in unison, the driver bobs up and down and a bell rings when pulled. The box is shown here so that you may know what the old style box looked like. Depending on the area, a toy in this condition will bring as much as twice the price of the same toy in "good" condition. 1951-54.

71 - #131 MILK WAGON - 9″ x 8″ x 6″ H. Milk Truck has plastic truck cab, wheels, bottles and carrier. Bell rings, driver's head turns side to side and carrier lifts out. 1965-72.

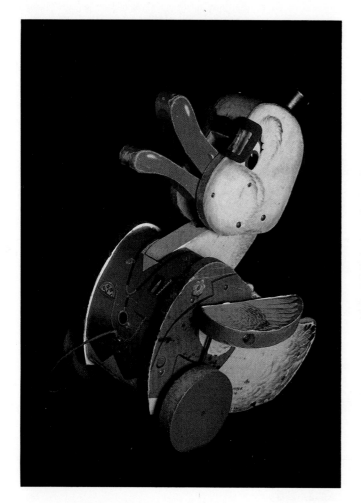

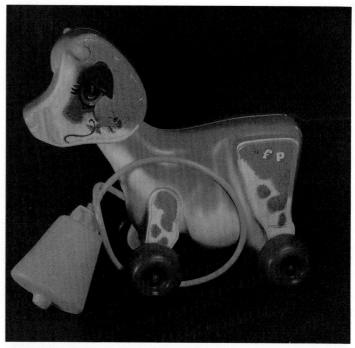

73 - #132 MOLLY MOO COW - Plastic cow with paper lithos, plastic wheels and vinyl squeeze bulb "bell." Spring tail. Hinged head raises and "moos" when bell is squeezed. 1972-78.

72 - #132 DR. DOODLE - 7″ x 9¹/₈″ H. Plastic spectacles. 1957-60. Courtesy of Sandy Witherspoon and Barbara B. Davis. Photo by Howard Davis.

74 - #132 PONY CHIME - 9¼" x 12" x 7¾" H. Twin horses pull musical metal cylinder on balloon wheels. Plastic tongue and bracket. 1965-67.

75 - #138 JACK-IN-THE-BOX PUPPET - 5½" Sq. x 6" H. Paper lithos on plastic box. Yellow button front releases top and puppet pops up. Pressing yellow lever moves puppet's mouth and eyes and makes him "talk." Cloth body. 1970-73.

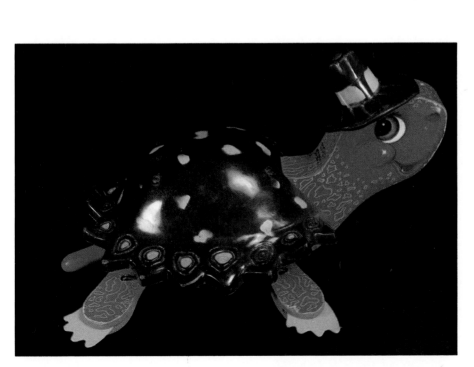

76 - #139 TUGGY TURTLE - 9" x 7" x 5¼" H. Vinyl feet, acetate hat and shell. Legs and tail move, inner xylophone plays. 1959-61.

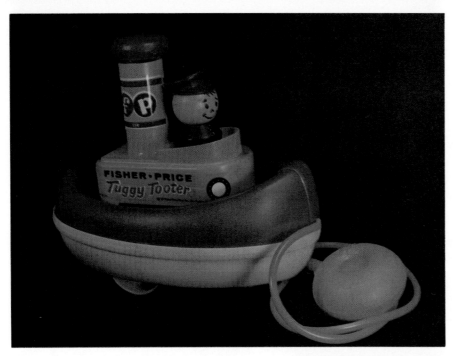

77 - #139 TUGGY TOOTER - 8″ x 4½″ x 7¼″ H. All plastic water or land toy. When bulb is squeezed, red top on smokestack raises and tugboat whistle sounds. 1967-73.

78 - #141 MINI BUS - 6½″ x 3½″ x 3¼″ H. All plastic with paper lithos. Comes with five passengers. 1969-present.

79 - #142 THREE MEN-IN-A-TUB - Plastic floor or tub toy has three variations: first had blue metal bell on top of center spring, this one has vinyl pennant and most recent model has inner bell with no center spring mast. Three plastic figures are weighted in the bottom and lift out. 1970-present.

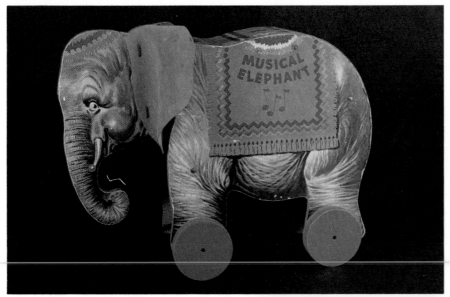

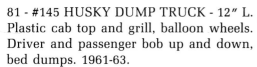

80 - #145 MUSICAL ELEPHANT - 10¼″ L. x 4¼″ x 8″ H. Suede lined, rubber fabric ears. Head and tail swing side to side; inside chimes. 1948-50. (Bead spring tail missing in photo.)

81 - #145 HUSKY DUMP TRUCK - 12″ L. Plastic cab top and grill, balloon wheels. Driver and passenger bob up and down, bed dumps. 1961-63.

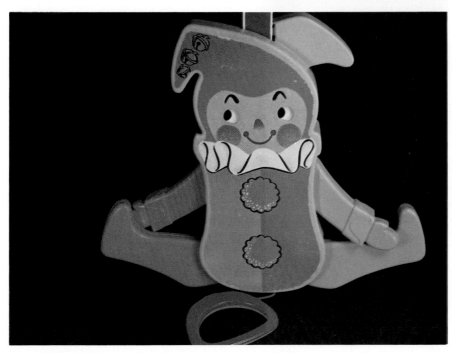

82 - #145 JOLLY JUMPING JACK - All plastic with paper lithos. Pulling handle activates squeaker, eyes, arms and legs. 1969-78.

83 - #146 PULL ALONG LACING SHOE -
9″ x 8″ H. Plastic shoe has wooden sole,
tongue and top. Figures have wooden
bodies and plastic heads. 1970-75.

84 - #150 TIMMY TURTLE - Acetate shell
conceals musical mechanism. 1953-56.

85 - #150 POP-UP PAL CHIME PHONE -
Plastic phone on wooden base. Buttons 1-9
play chimes; 0 opens top and shows girl
with phone. 1968-78.

86 - #151 HAPPY HIPPO - 15″ x 7½″ H. Plastic balloon wheels, bead spring tail and brown vinyl ears (missing in photo). Mouth gobbles up toys and holds them in hollow body. 1962-63.

87 - #151 GOLDILOCKS AND THE THREE BEARS PLAYHOUSE - 7″ x 6½″ x 7″ H. All plastic on wooden base. Goldilocks, Papa, Mama, and Baby Bear figures have wooden bodies, vinyl heads. 1967-70.

88 - #153 MESSAGE CENTER - 12½″ x 10″. Plastic desk has built-in phone dial, chalkboard and recessed area for chalk and eraser. 1978-present.

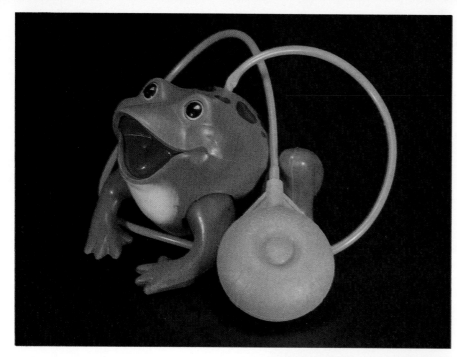

89 - #154 FRISKY FROG - Plastic frog jumps when yellow bulb is squeezed. 1971-present.

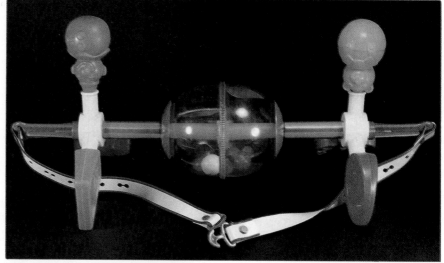

90 - #155 CRIB GYM - All plastic infant toy attaches across crib. 1973-present.

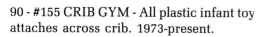

91 - #156 MUSIC BOX T.V. RADIO - 7¼" x 6" H. "Baa Baa Black Sheep" plays when knob is wound. Plastic knob and front panel. 1966-67.

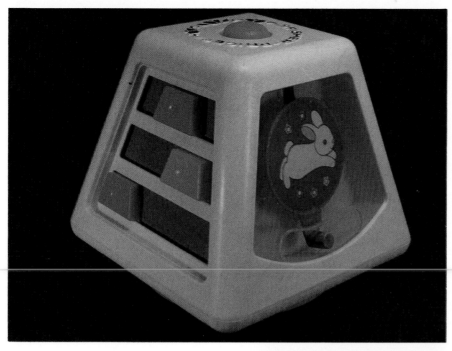

92 - #156 TURN AND LEARN ACTIVITY CENTER - All plastic infant toy sits on rotating base. 1978-present.

93 - #158 MUSIC BOX T.V. RADIO - 7¼″ x 6″ H. "Little Boy Blue" plays when knob is wound. Plastic knob and front plate. 1967.

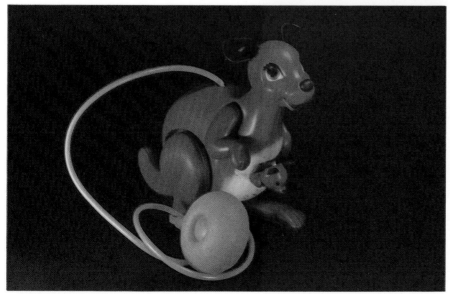

94 - #158 KATIE KANGAROO - Plastic kangaroo with brown vinyl ears, hops when yellow bulb is squeezed and makes a "sproing" sound. 1976-77.

95 - #161 LOOKY CHUG CHUG - Locomotive with metal bell that rings when pulled. Front cylinder is cardboard. 1949-52. Courtesy of Betty Jane Updike.

96 - #161 MUSIC BOX T.V. RADIO - 4″ x 7¼″ H. Plays ''The Old Woman Who Lived in a Shoe'' when knob is wound. Plastic knob and front plate, vinyl handle. Music box gears can be seen through clear plastic insert in back. 1968-70.

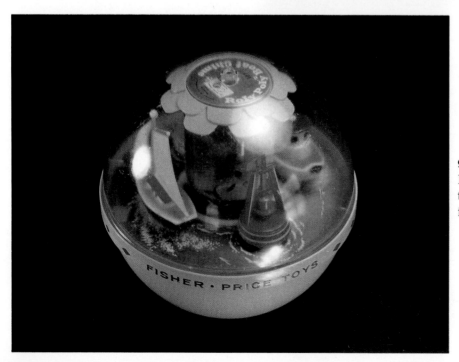

97 - #162 ROLY POLY BOAT CHIMES - 6″ Dia. Plastic chime ball has two boats and two bell buoys inside which rock back and forth. 1967-69.

98 - #164 MOTHER GOOSE - 9½″ x 6½″ x 11¼″ H. "Honking" mechanism conceal-ed in box construction body. Plastic neck, vinyl scarf and balloon wheels. Waddles side to side, head bobs, tail wags. 1964-66.

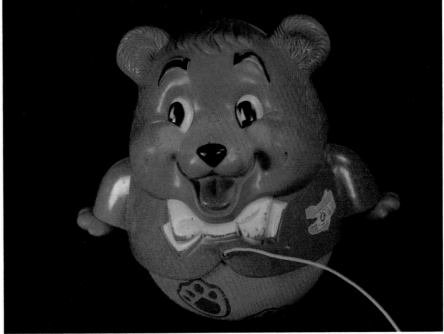

99 - #164 CHUBBY CUB, THE ROLL ALONG BEAR - 9″ H. Head and jacket are hollow plastic, separate hands attached (and often found missing). Weighted plastic ball with "beartracks" fits inside top half and rolls along on inner steel shaft. Chimes. 1969-72.

100 #165 ROLY POLY CHIME BALL - 6″ Dia. Plastic chime ball has two rocking horses and two rocking swans inside. 1965-present.

101 #166 BUCKY BURRO - 11¼″ L. x 7⅝″ H. Plastic ears, spring tail. 1955-57. Courtesy of Sandy Witherspoon and Barbara B. Davis. Photo by Howard Davis.

102 - #175 GOLD STAR STAGECOACH - 15½″ x 4¾″ x 8½″ H. Horses rock alternately back and forth, noisemaker under coach makes "pop-pop" sound. 1954-56.

103 - #177 OSCAR THE GROUCH IN HIS CAN - All plastic. When bulb is squeezed, Oscar pops out of his can. 1977-present.

104 - #178 and #179 SURPRISE CLOTH BOOKS, "WHAT'S IN MY POCKETS?" - 7" x 10". Five page cloth book with a pocket on front and back of each page. Each pocket has a different closure. (#178 for boys, #179 for girls.) 1971-1974.

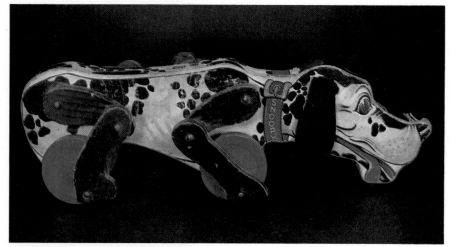

105 - #180 SNOOPY SNIFFER - 16½" L. x 5¼" H. Black felt ears are stapled on, as are black rubber feet. (Feet are missing from photo, as is the bead spring tail.) 1938-54.

106 - #181 SNOOPY SNIFFER - 14" L. Brown felt ears are stapled on. Bead spring tail, pin jointed plastic feet, plastic leash stapled to back of neck by gold ring. 1961-1980. Price in 1963 - $2.39.

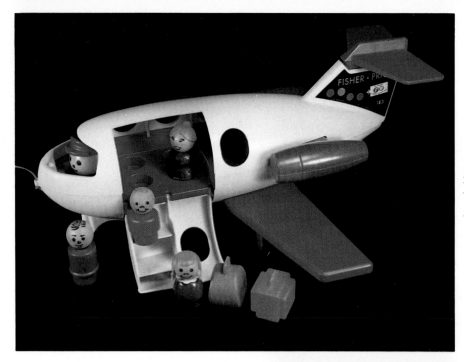

107 - #183 PLAY FAMILY FUN JET - 13¼″ x 11¾″ x 6″ H. Pilot's head turns from side to side. Playset includes two pieces of luggage and four figures. 1970-present.

108 - #184 TENNIS GAME - 23½″ x 11½″. Yellow squares operate rackets. Object is to hit ball into center hole. All plastic with paper lithos. 1976-78.

109 - #185 DONALD DUCK XYLOPHONE - 11″ x 6″ x 13″ H. Donald plays seven-key xylophone when pulled. 1938-43.

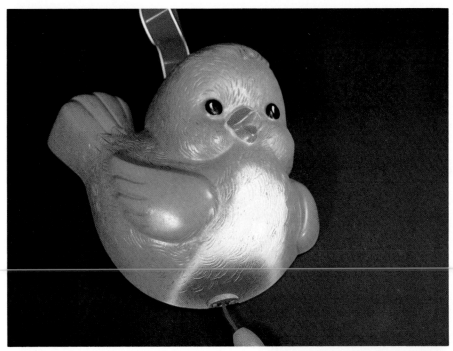

110 - #189 BLUEBIRD MUSIC BOX - 6" x 6" x 2" thick. Molded plastic bluebird has vinyl strap to attach to crib. Pulling string at bottom winds music box which plays "The Children's Prayer." 1969-79.

111 - #191 GOLDEN GULCH EXPRESS - 14" overall length. Piston rods, cowcatcher and "face," and rolling eyes are plastic. Cylinder on locomotive is cardboard. Coupler is black vinyl. 1961-62.

112 - #192 SCHOOL BUS - Plastic on wooden base, plastic balloon wheels. Driver's head turns side to side, eyes roll up and down. Seven passenger figures. 1965-present.

113 - #196 DOUBLE SCREEN COLOR T.V. MUSIC BOX - Plastic T.V. on wooden base. Music box plays "Hey Diddle Diddle;" picture cylinder revolves to show appropriate scenes. 1964-70. (#195, made in yellow plastic, played "Mary Had a Little Lamb." Made from 1965-68.)

114 - #197 STUFFINS FAMILY - Cloth hand puppets fit inside each other. The back of each one closes differently--lacing, snaps, zipper. (Mama Stuffins not shown.) 1971-72.

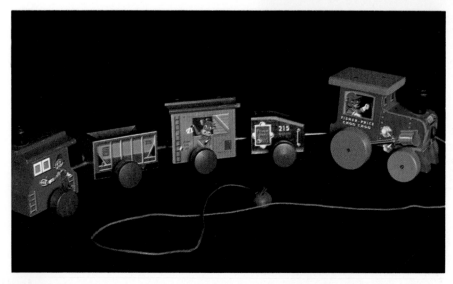

115 - #215 FISHER-PRICE CHOO-CHOO - 17″ x 3¼″ H. Steel connecting rods. 1955-57. Courtesy of Sandy Witherspoon and Barbara B. Davis. Photo by Howard Davis.

116 - #234 NIFTY STATION WAGON - 13½″ x 4½″ H. Wooden eye headlights roll when car is pulled. White plastic grill and roof supports. Four figures came with the car, not shown here. 1960-62.

117 - #303 EMERGENCY RESCUE TRUCK - Truck 8¾″ L. Set includes rescue truck with raising bucket and siren button, stretcher, oxygen tank, figures Tom and Nancy. 1975-78.

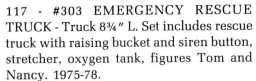

118 - #304 RUNNING BUNNY CART - 11″ x 4⁷⁄₈″ x 4″ H. Wooden wheels, original red pull string. 1957.

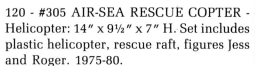

119 - #305 WALKING DUCK CART - 9″ x 4½″ L. x 7½″ H. Plastic feet and legs. Here's a good example of what happens when a pressure sticker is put on paper litho. 1957-64.

120 - #305 AIR-SEA RESCUE COPTER - Helicopter: 14″ x 9½″ x 7″ H. Set includes plastic helicopter, rescue raft, figures Jess and Roger. 1975-80.

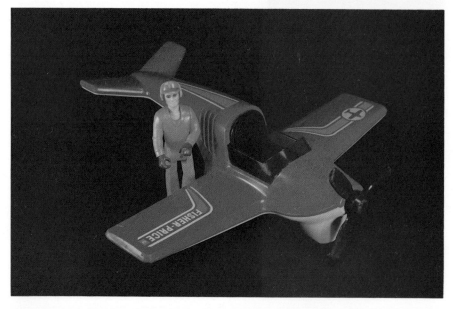

121 - #306 SPORT PLANE - Plane: 9½″ x 9½″. Pilot: 3¾″ H. Plastic airplane and vinyl figure with jointed arms, legs and neck. 1974-80.

122 - #307 ADVENTURE SERIES "WILDERNESS PATROL" - Airplane has 10″ wingspan. Set includes plane and pontoon boat, A.T.V., ranger figure Scott, pilot figure Gregg, woodsman figure Red (not shown), collie figure Scout, two sleeping bags and rope with hooks. 1976-79.

123 - #310 MICKEY MOUSE PUDDLE JUMPER - 6½″ x 5¼″ H. Car is hinged in the middle and has a diaphragm "clacker." This toy was sold in 1953 as part of a "Bargain Combination": a three-piece set, including the #325 Buzzy Bee and the #415 Super Jet Airplane. The three pieces sold for $1.55. 1953-56.

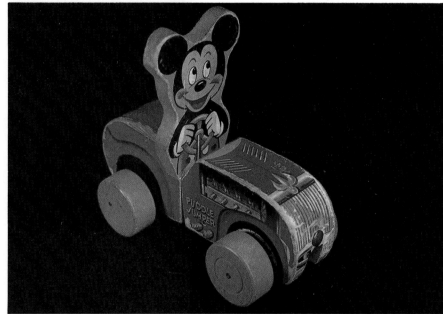

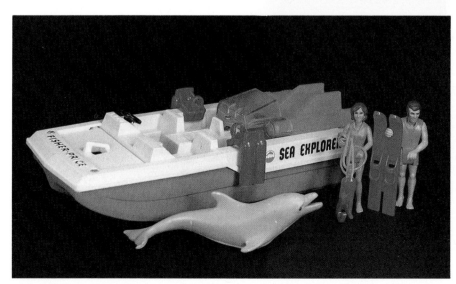

124 - #310 ADVENTURE SERIES "SEA EXPLORER" - Boat: 11¾″ L. Set includes Sea Explorer motorboat, sea sled, figures Dave and Mary, water skis, tow rope, two scuba tanks and dolphin figure Splash. 1976-80.

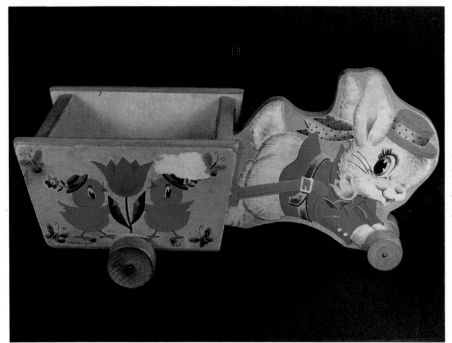

125 - #312 RUNNING BUNNY CART -
10¼" x 4" x 4½" H. Another example of
a toy which would be classified in "good"
condition except for the missing piece of
paper. ALWAYS check before you buy to
be certain the paper doesn't come off with
the price tag. 1960-64.

126 - #312 ADVENTURE SERIES "NOR-
THWOODS TRAILBLAZER" - Set includes jeep, canoe and two paddles, out-
board motor, cloth tent with vinyl
framework, and two figures, Brad and
Hawk. 1979.

127 - #325 BUZZY BEE - 6" x 5½" H. (to
tips of antennae). This little bee has plastic
wings, the first use of plastic by Fisher-
Price. 1950-56.

128 - #333 BUTCH THE PUP - (Shown with Suzie Seal for size.) 1951-54. Original price - 60¢. Courtesy of Sandy Witherspoon and Barbara B. Davis. Photo by Howard Davis.

129 - #359 LAND SPEED RACER - 8″ x 5″ x 2″ H. All plastic vehicle and vinyl figure with jointed arms, legs and neck. 1980-present.

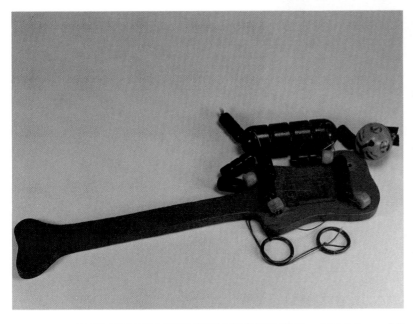

130 - #400 TAILSPIN TABBY POP-UP KRITTER - 10½″ L. paddle. Series of painted wooden beads strung on linen strings running down through holes in paddle base which form a cat when strings are pulled taut. (Tail missing in second photo.) The first paddles were round; this shape was a later one. 1931-38.

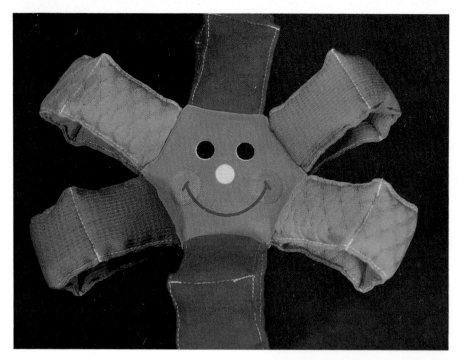

131 - #410 FUN FLOWER - Infant toy is cloth covered foam with inside squeaker. 1973-79.

132 - #411 FLOATING FAMILY - Six-piece floating plastic set. 1975-present.

133 - #413 HEY DIDDLE DIDDLE MOBILE - Counterweighted plastic figures from nursery rhymes hang from yellow metal bar and hook which attaches to side of crib or playpen. 1976-78.

134 - #414 FIRST BLOCKS - Hollow plastic shape blocks fit through shape sorter top. 1977-present.

135 - #416 SQUEAK-A-BOO - Fabric and plush toy has inside rattle and squeakers in "ears." Fingers fit through loops in back. 1973-79.

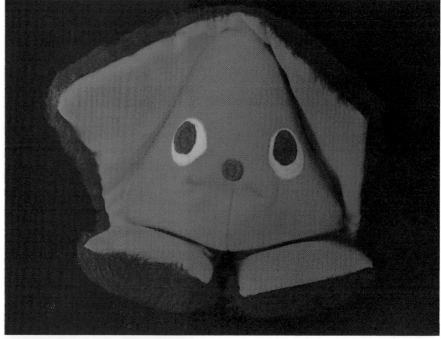

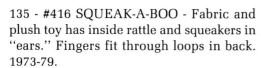

136 - #417 CLICK 'N' CLATTER CAR - All plastic flip-over car with chunky figure. 1975-80.

137 - #418 FREDDY BEAR - 12″ H. Urethane foam stuffed teddy bear has plush fur, vinyl eyes and inside squeaker. 1975-80.

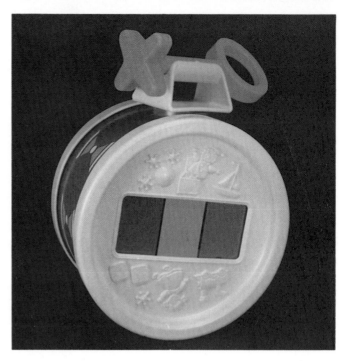

138 - #421 XYLO DRUM - Plastic drum has three metal xylophone keys and vinyl "drumstick." (Style of drumstick was changed around 1980.) 1977-present.

139 - #423 JUMPING JACK SCARECROW - Similar to #145 Jolly Jumping Jack. 1978-80.

140 - #424 FLOWER RATTLE - Old: 7½″ L.; new: 7″ L. Original version of the all-plastic rattle. Most recent one has green handle instead of red ball. 1973-present.

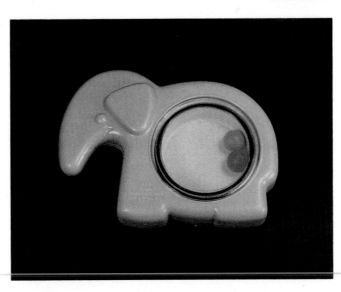

141 - #426 SQUEAKY BEAR - 4½″ x 4½″. Plastic toy with vinyl head and feet, vinyl "tummy" squeaker. 1977-80.

142 - #429 LOOK AT ME ELEPHANT RATTLE - Plastic rattle has mirror on one side. 1976-80.

143 - #430 ANIMAL RING - Two styles of the vinyl teething ring. Old Style: 1976-77; new, 1977-80.

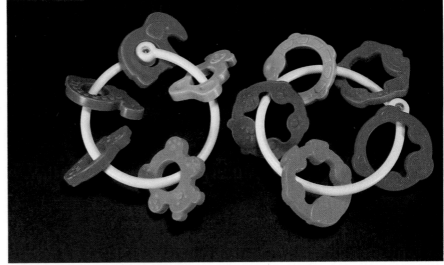

144 - #436, 437, 438 ANIMAL GRABBERS - 3″ x 4½″ x 5″ approx. Terry cloth covered urethane foam infant toys have inside squeakers. 1978-present.

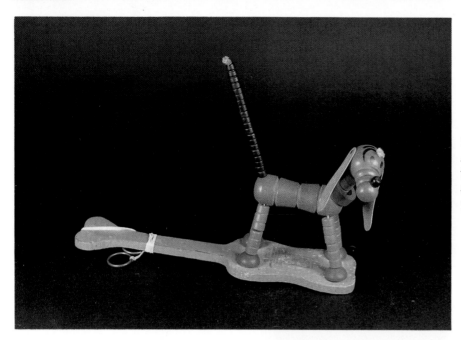

145 - #440 PLUTO POP-UP KRITTER - Another in the line of Pop-Up Kritter Toys, this one is Mickey Mouse's dog, Pluto. See #400 Tailspin Tabby for description. 1936-49.

146 - #444 PUFFY ENGINE - 6″ x 4″ H. Another early use of plastic, the arm pistons in this toy are plastic. 1951-54. Courtesy of Betty Jane Updike.

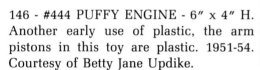

147 - #444 QUEEN BUZZY BEE - 6″ x 6″ H. This red and white color version of the familiar current toy also had a blue vinyl crown. Plastic wings. 1959-62.

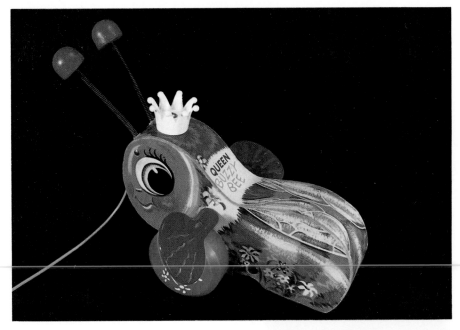

148 - #444 QUEEN BUZZY BEE - 6″ x 6″ H. This is the more familiar version. Plastic wings and wheels, vinyl crown. Earlier bees have wooden wheels and antennae beads; later ones are both plastic. 1963-present.

149 - #445 HOT DOG WAGON - 10¾″ L. x 7″ H. Wooden bead tail rings bell when toy is pulled. 1940-41.

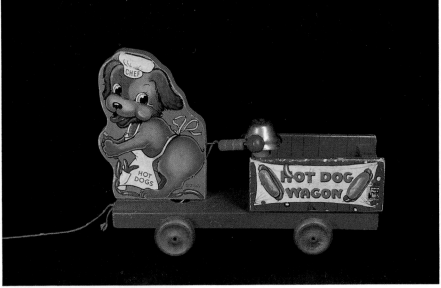

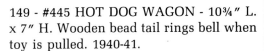

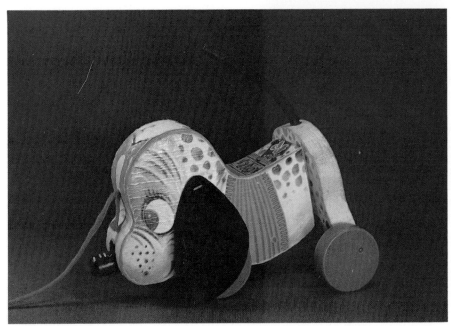

150 - #445 "NOSEY" PUP - 6″ x 4″ H. Black felt ears, 3½″ long black vinyl tail. Back leg section is hinged, causing tail to wag when pulled. Nose moves in and out, barking sound. 1956-59.

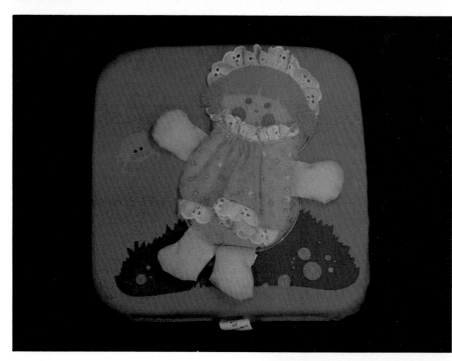

151 - #447 LITTLE MISS MUFFET DOLL & PILLOW - 9½″ sq. Fabric covered urethane foam. Removable doll has yarn hair and inside squeaker. 1977-80.

152 - #448 MINI COPTER - 6¼″. Plastic top and tail rotors, plastic wheels. 1971-80.

153 - #450 DONALD DUCK CHOO-CHOO - 9″ x 7¼″ H. Front of engine is cardboard cylinder with metal front. Metal bell. (Bell clapper missing.) 1946-49. Courtesy of Betty Jane Updike.

154 - #451 SHAKE 'N' ROLL RATTLE - 6¼″ H. All plastic with mirror in one end. 1973-79.

155 - #460 SUZIE SEAL - 5½″ x 7″ H. In this "herd of seals," the one with yellow front wheels and no bell is the #460 Suzie; 1961-64. The one with the umbrella is #623; 1964-65. The next one, with ball and bell, is #621; 1965-66. The one with the bead spring on its nose may have been a variation of #621. Price in 1963 - 67¢.

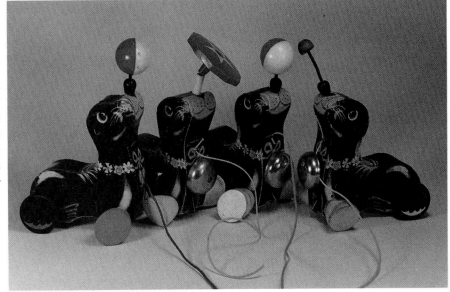

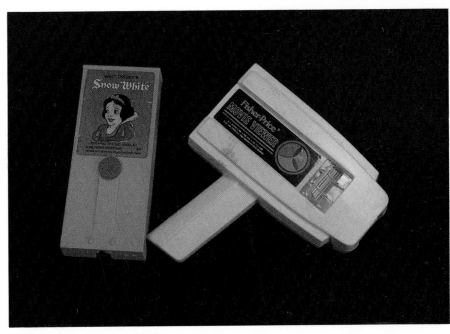

156 - #460 MOVIE VIEWER - Hand-held plastic case holds movie cartridges. Handle on opposite side advances film strip. 1973-present.

59

157 - #462 BARKY - 5″ x 4½″ H. Bulldog has vinyl tongue and ears. Hemispherical wooden eyes roll up and down when pulled. 1958-60. Courtesy of Kurt L. Peterson.

158 - #464 GRAN'PA FROG - 6″ x 5″ H. Green feet on back wheels are plastic. Hemispherical wooden eyes move up and down. Frog-like gait and "garrumph" sound when pulled. 1956-58.

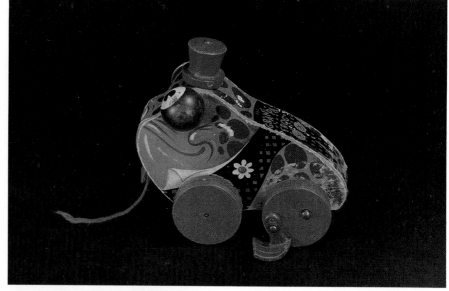

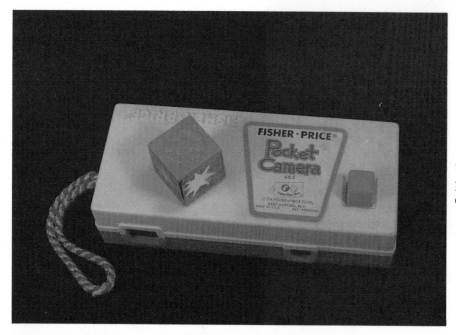

159 - #464 POCKET CAMERA - Plastic "camera" has cord handle. When button is pushed, flash cube turns and picture inside changes. 1974-present.

160 - #473 MERRY MUTT - 7½″ x 8″. Dog plays two-key metal xylophone when pulled. 1949.

161 - #476 MICKEY MOUSE DRUMMER - Mickey's drum is cardboard cylinder with metal top. He plays drum when pulled. 1941-43 and 1946-49.

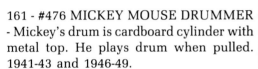

162 - #476 COOKIE PIG - 5½″ x 4¾″ H. Hat, ears, tail and wheels are vinyl. Tail spins when pulled. 1965-70.

163 - #485 MICKEY MOUSE CHOO-CHOO - 8½″ x 3½″ x 7″ H. Front of locomotive is cardboard cylinder with metal front. Metal bell. (Bead on mallet missing.) 1949-53. Courtesy of Gene and Anita Brownfield.

164 - #495 SLEEPY SUE - 6¼″ x 3½″ x 3½″ H. This little turtle has vinyl hat, tail and shell. Tail wags when pulled. 1963. Price in 1963 - 67¢.

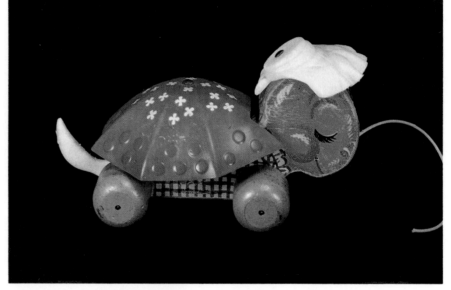

165 - #540 GRANNY DUCK - 1939-42. Courtesy of Jean Couch. Photo by Jerry Couch.

166 - #549 TOY LUNCH KIT - 5″ x 2″ x 4½″ H. Paper lithos on plastic lunch box and thermos. 1972-79.

167 - #605 MAYOR GOODGRUB MOLE - Set includes storybook *Mayor Goodgrub's Very Important Day* and Mayor Goodgrub Mole squeaking finger puppet made of fabric and vinyl. 1980-83.

168 - #606 BRAMBLE BEAVER - Set includes storybook *Bramble Beaver's Bright Idea* and Bramble Beaver squeaking finger puppet made of fabric and vinyl. 1980-83.

169 - #607 VERY BLUE BIRD - Set includes storybook *The Seasons With V. B. Bird* and Very Blue Bird squeaking finger puppet made of fabric and vinyl. 1980-83.

170 - #616 PATCH PONY - 7″ x 8″ H. Ears and balloon wheels are vinyl. Wooden bead spring tail. Galloping gait with "clippety-clop" sound. 1961-65. Price in 1963 - $1.18.

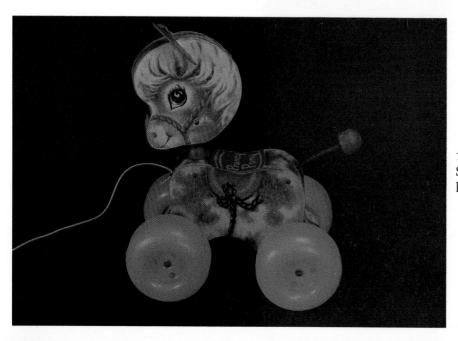

171 - #617 PRANCY PONY - 7″ x 8″ H. Same toy as #616 with different paper lithos applied. 1965-66.

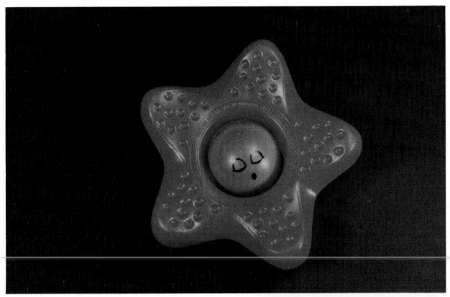

172 - #623 SANDY STARFISH - Vinyl infant rattle shows blue asleep face on one side, yellow awake face on the other. 1979-80.

173 - #624 SAM THE CLAM - Heavy yellow plastic shell holds pink vinyl clam. When squeezed, clam takes in water. Another squeeze squirts it out. 1977-present.

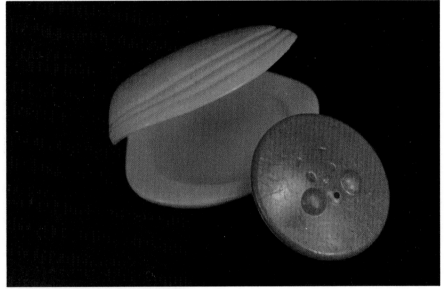

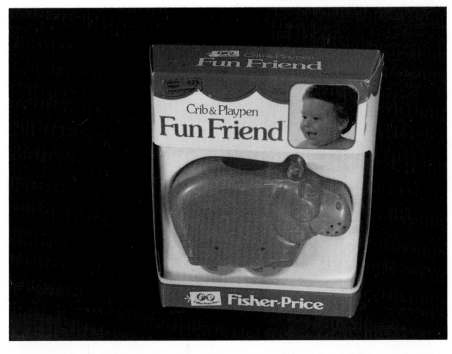

174 - #625 HENRY HIPPO - 5″ L. Hollow plastic floor or water toy. 1979-present.

175 - #626 PLAYFUL PUPPY - 6½″ x 5″ H. Vinyl tail. Vinyl ears attached to front wheels make head turn from side to side when pulled. 1963-66. Price in 1963 - 78¢.

176 - #628 TUG-A-BUG - 5¼″ x 4″ x 3″ H. All plastic, even bead spring antennae. 1974-77.

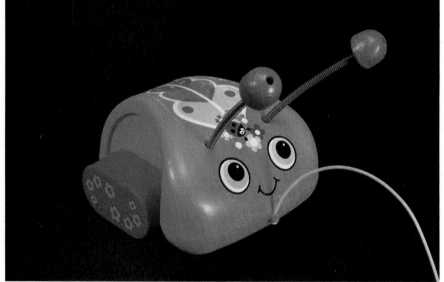

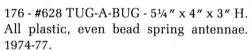

177 - #629 MIGHTY TRACTOR - 5½″ x 5½″ x 5¾″ H. Vinyl hat brim, smokestack and rear wheels. Farmer rocks side to side and turns head when pulled. 1962-68. Price in 1963 - 78¢.

178 - #634 TINY TEDDY - Bead spring mallets play three-keyed xylophone. (Red disc on end of string not original.) 1955-57. Courtesy of Beth Crain.

179 - #635 TINY TEDDY - 6″ x 7¼″ H. Bead spring mallets play three-keyed xylophone. 1962-66.

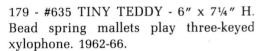

180 - #636 TINY TEDDY - 6¼″ x 8″ H. Bead spring mallets play three-keyed xylophone. 1958-62.

181 - #637 MILK CARRIER - Vinyl bottles and carrier. 1966-present. (This carrier is similar to the turquoise one that fits into the back of the #131 Milk Wagon.)

182 - #638 LUNCH BOX - $7^7/_8''$ x $7^3/_8''$ x $2^3/_8''$. Plastic lunch box with matching thermos. 1979-present.

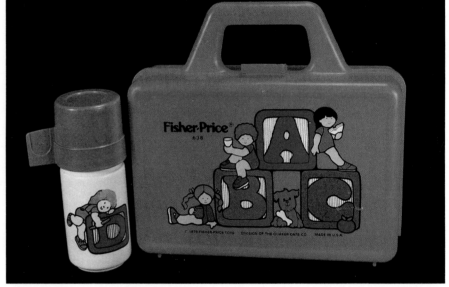

183 - #641 TOOT-TOOT ENGINE - 6'' L. Vinyl cab, cowcatcher, and connecting rods on wheels. Clicking sound when pulled. 1962-64. Price in 1963 - 78¢.

184 - #642 DINKEY ENGINE - 6″ L. Same toy as #641 with different paper lithos. 1959. (Original price, 98¢, stamped on bottom.)

185 - #642 SMOKIE ENGINE - 6″ L. Same toy as #642 with only a name change this time. 1960-62.

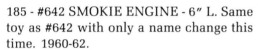

186 - #642 BOB ALONG BEAR - 6″ x 7″ H. All plastic. Arms rotate and balls inside hemispheres hop around. 1978-present.

187 - #643 TOOT-TOOT ENGINE - 6″ L. Again, the same basic toy as #641 and #642 with a paper litho change and change in color of the plastic parts. The back wheels are wooden on early ones, plastic on later ones. 1964-present.

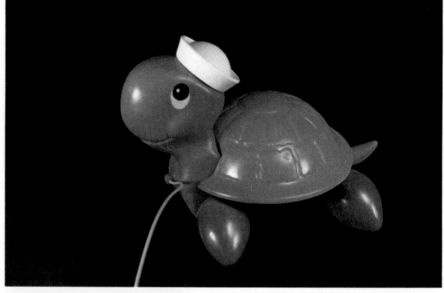

188 - #644 TAG ALONG TURTLE - Small, all-plastic turtle wags tail when pulled. 1977-present.

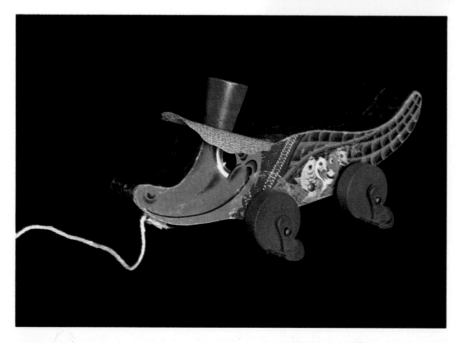

189 - #653 ALLIE GATOR - 10$\frac{1}{8}$″ x 4$\frac{1}{4}$″ H. Hat brim is vinyl, green feet are plastic. (Pull string not original.) 1960-62. Courtesy of Sandy Witherspoon and Barbara B. Davis. Photo by Howard Davis.

190 - #656 BOSSY BELL - 6″ x 6″ H. Tail and horns are vinyl; metal bell. Tail spings and bell rings when pulled. 1959-63. Price in 1963 - 78¢.

191 - #658 LADYBUG - 8″ x 4½″ H. Plastic dome shell revolves and chimes. 1961-63.

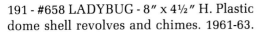

192 - #659 PUZZLE PUPPY - 3¾″ x 8¼″ H. Eight piece hollow plastic fit-together puzzle for toddlers. 1976-present.

193 - #662 MERRY MOUSEWIFE - 6¾″ x 2½″ x 5¾″ H. Cap, tail, hands and broom are vinyl. "Sweeps" side to side when pulled. 1963. Price in 1963 - 78¢.

194 - #677 PICNIC BASKET - Basket: 6″ x 4¼″ x 4″ H. with handle down. All plastic basket, plate, spoon and bear thermos; fabric red gingham cloth. 1975-79.

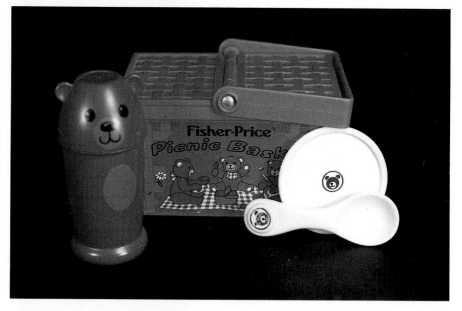

195 - #678 KRIS KRICKET - Legs move and a cricket sound is made when pulled. 1955-57. Courtesy of Jessie Hanson.

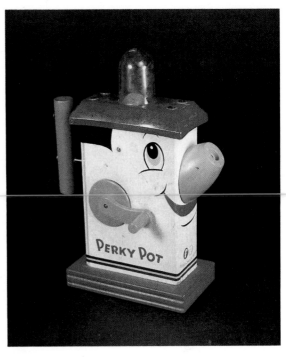

196 - #684 MARY'S LITTLE LAMB - 7″ x 6½″ H. Vinyl ears, tail and balloon wheels. Bell rings and tail wags. 1964-65.

197 - #686 PERKY POT - 5¼″ x 2¼″ x 6¾″ H. Plastic percolator top and winding handle. Turning handle makes wooden bead pop up inside top. 1959-60.

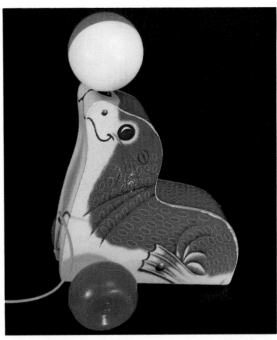

198 - #693 LITTLE SNOOPY - Vinyl ears and balloon wheels, bead spring tail. 1965-present.

199 - #694 SUZY SEAL - 4½″ x 4½″ H. Vinyl wheels, spinning plastic ball. 1979-present.

200 - #695 PINKY PIG - 7″ x 5½″ H. Vinyl ears, plastic umbrella. Umbrella spins and hemispherical eyes roll up and down when pulled. 1956-58.

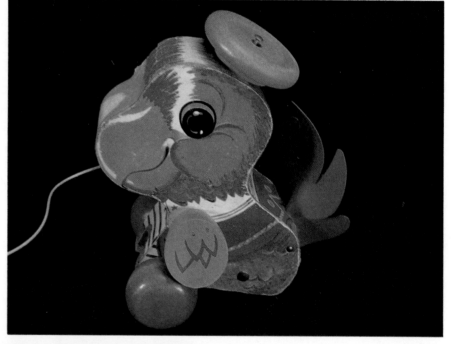

201 - #698 TALKY PARROT - 4½″ L. x 6″ H. Vinyl tail. Wings roll and squawking sound is made when pulled. 1963-64. Price in 1963 - 78¢.

202 - #703 BUNNY ENGINE - 10″ x 4¼″ H. Front cylinder is cardboard with metal end, metal bell. 1954-56. Courtesy of Betty Jane Updike.

203 - #705 MINI SNOWMOBILE - 7″ x 3″ H. Plastic snowmobile with paper lithos pulls smaller snow sled. 1970-73. Accessory piece for the Play Family A-Frame.

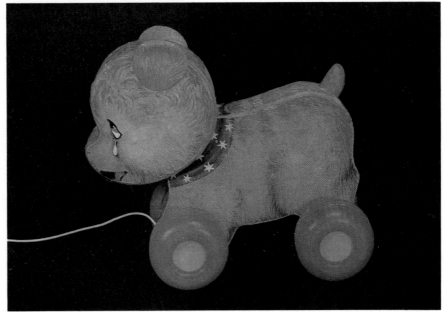

204 - #711 CRY BABY BEAR - 8½″ x 7½″ H. Ears, tail and wheels are vinyl. Paper lithos over plastic head. Head nods up and down and bear "cries" when pulled. 1966-69. Paper lithos do not adhere as well to plastic parts as they do wooden; therefore, toys like these are most often found missing paper lithos.

205 - #712 TEDDY TOOTER - 6¾″ x 4¾″ x 9½″ H. Horn and inner "blowing" mechanism are plastic. Hands, head and horn raise and lower when pulled; horn "toots." 1957-59.

206 - #715 DUCKY FLIP FLAP - Duck: 11″ x 5½″ wingspan. Handle: 21″ L. Vinyl wheels originally had yellow vinyl "feet" in the slots on outside of the wheel which "flip-flapped" when toy was pushed. Orange plastic ball on end of handle. 1964-65.

207 - #718 TOW TRUCK AND CAR - 4″ x 3¼″ x 3¼″ H. The red and white parts of this tow truck are plastic. (Hook and car missing from photo) 1968-70.

208 - #719 CUDDLY CUB - Roly poly bear toy is fabric and plush fabric. Inside chime. 1973-77.

209 - #720 FIRE ENGINE - 9″ x 3½″ H. Plastic front windshield and bumper, ladder and support, and wheels. Cord hose, metal bell. Firemen figures are also plastic in this example. Driver's head turns side to side and bell rings when pulled. 1968-present.

211 - #724 JOLLY JALOPY - 7″ x 7″ H. All yellow parts are plastic; plastic balloon wheels. Clown's head is on a metal spring. 1965-78.

210 - #722 MUSICAL PUSH CHIME - Metal bracket holds metal chiming cylinder. Wheels are paper lithos on wood, handle is painted wood. Later ones had plastic ball on handle, slightly different lithography on cylinder and on wheels. 1950-67.

213 - #728 BUDDY BULLFROG - 6½″ x 6″ H. Frog jumps realistically and "croaks" when pulled. 1959-60. Courtesy of Betty Jane Updike.

212 - #727, #728 and #797 - HORSE, BEAR & RABBIT LITTLE LACE UPS - These are flat plastic forms that come with two lacing cords each. 1980-present.

214 - #730 RACING ROWBOAT - 7¾″ x 4½″ H. Plastic arms and oars, vinyl pennant on spring staff. 1952-53. Courtesy of Betty Jane Updike.

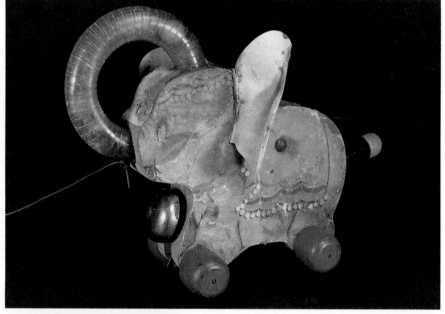

215 - #735 JUGGLING JUMBO - 10″ x 3½″ x 7¼″ H. Plastic crank on side, plastic trunk and vinyl ears. Crank "shoots" balls through trunk and rings bell. Bead spring tail wags when pulled. 1958-59. Price in 1958 - $1.98. (This is a VERY POOR example. The paper litho is in bad shape. The vinyl ear has been damaged and the crank no longer works. Really a GREAT toy when found in good shape.)

216 - #736 HUMPTY DUMPTY - All plastic toy whose arms revolve when pulled. 1972-79.

217 - #738 SHAGGY ZILO - 8½″ x 9″ H. Bear plays four-keyed metal xylophone with bead spring mallets when pulled. 1960-62.

218 - #739 POODLE ZILO - 8½″ x 7¾″ H. Poodle plays three-keyed metal xylophone with bead spring mallets when pulled. 1961-64.

219 - #740 GIANT ROCK-A-STACK - This large version of the common stacking toy has screw-on top ball. All plastic. 1961-80.

220 - #741 TEDDY ZILO - 9″ x 8¼″ H. This Zilo toy has three-keyed metal xylophone and plastic wheels. 1966-67. Courtesy of Betty Jane Updike.

221 - #745 ELSIE'S DAIRY - 9¾″ x 6⁷/₈″ H. Beau-Regard, the driver, plays the bell as toy is pulled. (Clear milk bottles not shown.) 1948-49. Courtesy of Sandy Witherspoon and Barbara B. Davis. Photo by Howard Davis.

222 - #747 CHATTER TELEPHONE - Should be familiar to all, as this is Fisher-Price's all-time No. 1 best seller. Since over thirty million of these toys have been sold, they are extremely common. Earlier ones had wooden wheels, and the most recent ones have a spiral cord on the receiver. 1961-present.

223 - #752 TEDDY ZILO - 9″ x 4¾″ x 11″ H. This Zilo bear has a five-keyed metal xylophone to play. (Small piece of original red pull string still attached.) 1946-50. Courtesy of Lisa Saults.

224 - #755 JUMBO ROLLO - 9½″ x 7″ x 9″ H. Legs pedal, arms move and beads rattle around in rear cylinder cage. 1951-52. Courtesy of Betty Jane Updike.

225A and 225B - #757 HUMPTY DUMPTY - 10¼″ x 10½″ H. An unusual pull toy, Humpty is hinged at hips. Metal bell on each hand. 1957-58. Courtesy of Betty Jane Updike.

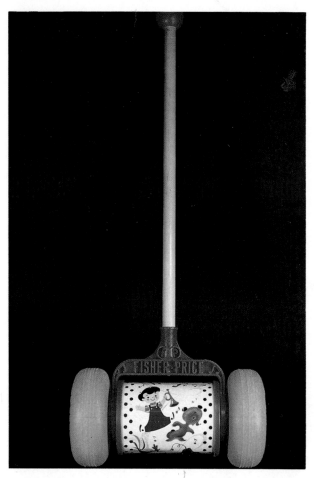

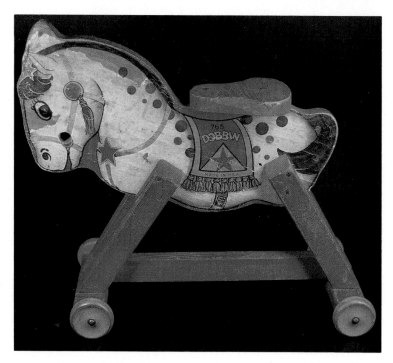

227 - #765 DANDY DOBBIN - 12½″ x 12″ H. Note the small size of this horse in comparison to most ride-on toys. 1941-46.

226 - #757 MELODY PUSH CHIME - 9″ x 23¼″ total height. Metal litho cylinder holds chiming mechanism. Plastic bracket and end knob, vinyl balloon wheels. 1963-present.

228 - #767 GABBY DUCK - Small pull toy moves with a waddling gait, opens and closes bill when quacking. 1952-53.

229 - #765 DONALD DUCK - 5¾″ x 8″ H. Plastic legs and "stirrups." Donald runs along, swinging his arms. c. 1950. Courtesy of Betty Jane Updike.

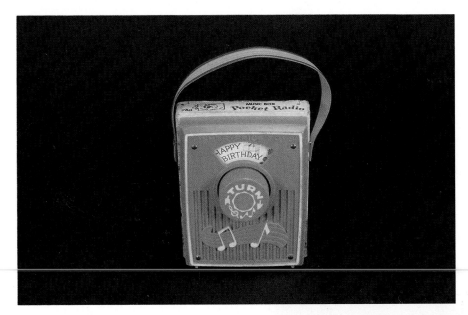

230 - #768 MUSIC BOX POCKET RADIO - 4½″ x 3½″. One in the series of pocket radios, all different colors with different paper lithos and playing a different tune. This one plays "Happy Birthday To You." 1971-76.

231 - #773 TIP TOE TURTLE - All plastic except head and neck. Feet walk, chimes when pulled. 1962-77.

232 - #776 GABBY GOOFIES - 13″ x 5½″ H. Plastic rotating wings and black vinyl hat brim. Steel connecting rods. 1960-63.

233 - #777 TEDDY ZILO - 9″ x 4½″ x 10½″ H. Bear plays five-keyed metal xylophone with bead spring mallets. 1950-51.

234 - #777 SQUEAKY THE CLOWN - 7″ L. x 9″ H. Plastic neck ruffle. Clown bounces along the floor on his bottom. 1958-59. Price in 1958 - $1.59. Courtesy of Sandy Witherspoon and Barbara B. Davis. Photo by Howard Davis.

235 - #777 GABBY GOOFIES - This style change from the #776 model shown earlier includes substitution of vinyl neck ruffle for hat brim, white paddle wings as well as colored ones, colored wheels instead of black, and gold-flecked paint job. 1963-70.

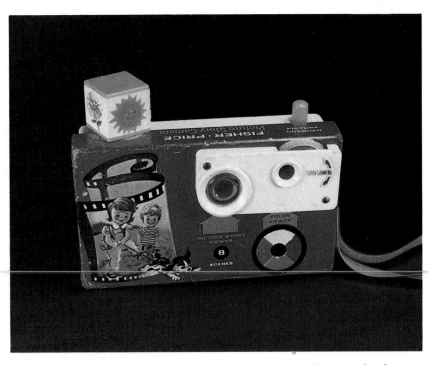

236 - #779 MUSIC BOX POCKET RADIO - Same toy as #768, but this one plays "Yankee Doodle." 1975.

237 - #784 PICTURE STORY CAMERA - 5" x 3". This is a back view. Front is white plastic with yellow plastic "focusing lens." Vinyl wrist loop. Pressing yellow button on top turns flash cube and advances film strip. 1967-73.

238 - #786 PERKY PENGUIN - 8" H. All plastic. When bulb is squeezed, eyes roll, mouth opens and makes a cry. 1973-75.

239 - #788 CORN POPPER - 8¼" x 6" H.; 17½" handle. Plastic dome, balloon wheels, balls, "popping" mechanism and ball at end of handle. (Version #785, made 1957-62, has wooden wheels and balls as well as a different shaped plastic knob at end of handle.) 1963-present.

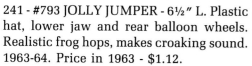

240 - #792 MUSIC BOX RADIO - 5″ x 4″ x 1½″ thick. All plastic with paper litho on back. 1979-80.

241 - #793 JOLLY JUMPER - 6½″ L. Plastic hat, lower jaw and rear balloon wheels. Realistic frog hops, makes croaking sound. 1963-64. Price in 1963 - $1.12.

242 - #794 BIG BILL PELICAN - 9″ x 7¾″ H. White vinyl feathers on head, red plastic bill and feet. Bill opens and closes when pulled. 1961-68.

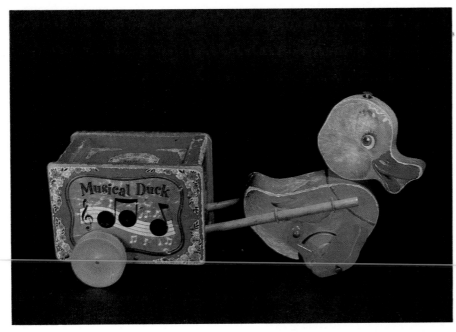

243 - #795 MUSICAL DUCK - 13″ x 6½″ H. Plastic legs and feet. Three-key metal xylophone concealed in cart plays when pulled. 1952-55.

244 - #799 DUCKIE TRANSPORT - 1937-38. Courtesy of Jean Couch. Photo by Jerry Couch.

245 - #799 QUACKY FAMILY - 13¼″ x 5″ H. Bills are plastic, steel rod connectors. 1940-58. The toy made in the early 40s had rubber connectors which allowed the family to be taken apart and put back together.

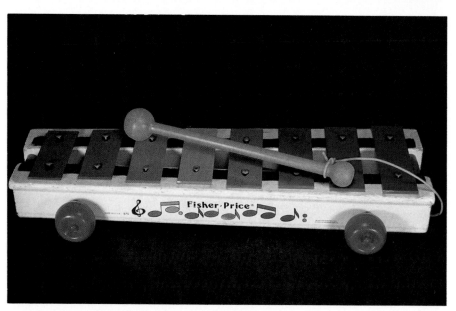

247 - #870 PULL-A-TUNE XYLOPHONE - 14″ x 5″ x 2¼″ H. Eight-keyed metal xylophone with three concealed mallets which play when pulled. Early ones had wooden wheels and a wooden mallet for child to use. Both are plastic in recent ones. Came with color keyed music folder. 1957-present.

246 - #855 MISS PIGGY HAND PUPPET - The well-known Jim Henson "Muppet" character. All synthetic material, foam and vinyl except eyes, which are a harder plastic. 1979-present.

249 - #875 LOOKY PUSH CAR - 6½″ x 8″ x 7″ H., 20″ handle. Difficult to find in good shape. Plastic bumper, fenders, windshield and balloon tires. Also plastic "steering wheel" with vinyl beep button in the center. Eyes roll up and down, "brr-rumm" noisemaker. 1962-69. Price in 1963 - $2.59.

248 - #890 MISS PIGGY - 14″ H. Urethane foam stuffed fabric figure has vinyl head, rooted hair, removable dress and headband. 1980.

250A, 250B and 250C - #900 BIG PER-FORMING CIRCUS - Wagon with top is 15″ x 7″ x 11″ H. Thirty-piece set consists of circus wagon with removable top (first photo), 11 basic performers which have plastic arms and legs (second photo), and the following equipment (third photo): four red wooden ladders with plastic rungs, three yellow plastic ladder connectors, four yellow wooden poles, one yellow plastic trapeze, one yellow plastic aerial spinner, a two-piece center ring 11″ in diameter, a black wooden tub and a red wooden ball for seal's nose (not shown.) 1962-70. Price in 1963 - $9.99. (Paper lithos missing from wagon wheels.)

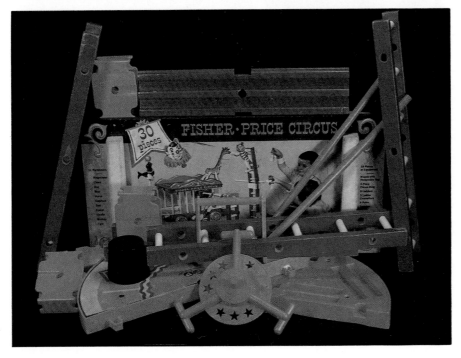

251A, 251B and 251C - #902 JR. CIRCUS SET - This set uses some of the same pieces as the big circus; but it has a 7″ diameter, one-piece center ring. Set consists of the same 11 basic performers, two ladders instead of four, two ladder connectors instead of three, two poles instead of four, a trapeze, aerial spinner, black tub and red ball (not shown.) First photo: original box; second photo: entire set; third photo: equipment only. 1963-70. Original price, $4.88.

252 - #905 THIS LITTLE PIG . . . - 13″ x 3″ x 3″ H. Five polyethylene pigs on plastic wheels. Each pig "oinks" when squeezed, first pig also rattles. 1959-62. Pigs may be either all pink or multi-colored.

253 - #909 PLAY FAMILY ROOMS - 12″ x 18½″ x 4¾″ H. Paper lithos over hard board main play piece. Components include: four play people and one puppy; lime green table and four chairs; barbeque grill; blue TV set; two red or blue chairs; one red and one blue armchair; red or blue coffee table; yellow kitchen sink, stove and refrigerator; white bathtub, scale, commode and sink (sink not shown); wading pool (not shown) and flowered patio umbrella table and two chairs (not shown). c. 1972-1974.

254 - #910 CHANGE-A-TUNE PIANO - Eight-key music box piano has plastic keyboard and knob on side. One of three tunes can be played, depending upon which pictures shows: "The Muffin Man," "Pop! Goes the Weasel," and "This Old Man." 1969-72.

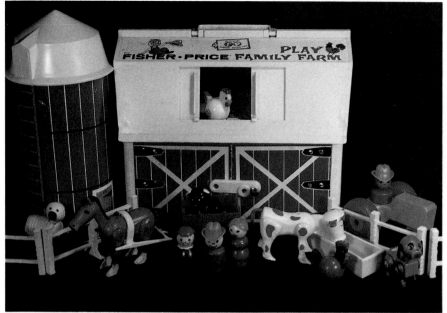

255 - #915 PLAY FAMILY FARM - Barn: 11″ x 6⁷/₈″ x 8¼″ H. This was the first multi-piece "Play Family" playset made by Fisher-Price. Set includes white plastic and pressed wood barn, cardboard silo with white plastic top, tractor, hay wagon and harness, four fence sections, two chickens, cow, horse, sheep, pig, dog, water trough and four play-family figures. 1968-present.

256 - #923 PLAY FAMILY SCHOOL - Set includes main schoolhouse with fold-down side, two trays of magnetic letters and numbers, five figures (teacher and four students), four school desks, teacher's desk and chair, swing, slide and whirl-around. (Small box of chalk and an eraser not shown.) 1971-present.

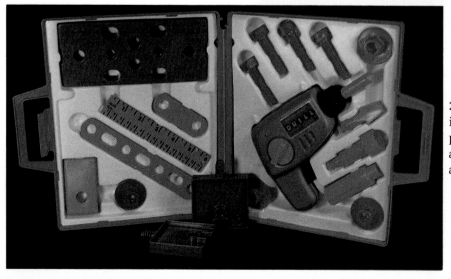

257 - #924 TOOL KIT - Case: 10″ x 10″. Set includes plastic tool box and snap-in white plastic tool holders, wind-up drill, four nuts and bolts, 6″ ruler, three-piece worktable, assorted drill tips and plastic links. 1977-83.

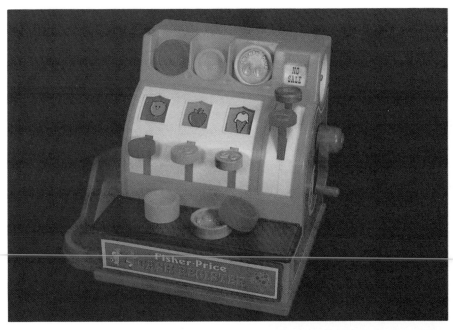

258 - #926 CASH REGISTER - 10″ x 9″ x 7½″. All plastic cash register with paper lithos. Includes six coins. 1974-present.

259 - #928 FIRE STATION - All plastic playset includes station building, fire truck, ambulance, fire chief car, two-piece ladder, three firemen, dog, two barricades, two truck braces and gray building. 1980-present.

260 - #929 PLAY FAMILY NURSERY SCHOOL - Base: 13¾″ x 10″ x 5½″ H.; bus: 6¼″ L. Lift-off roof is paper lithos over cardboard and flips over to form playground. Set includes plastic main school with carrying handle, six figures, sink, commode, kitchen sink, stove, round table, four chairs, painting easel, teeter-totter, slide, whirl-around and school bus. 1978-present.,

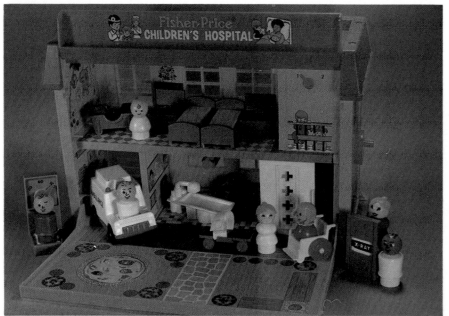

261 - #931 PLAY FAMILY CHILDREN'S HOSPITAL - Main piece is hospital, one side of which opens down. Crank on side operates elevator, garage door on back side opens for ambulance. Set includes seven figures (man, woman, child, baby, nurse, white doctor and black doctor), ambulance, stretcher, wheelchair, scale, x-ray machine, sink, operating table, two beds, two "bed-pans", infant bed and white screen (not shown.) 1976-78.

262 - #932 AMUSEMENT PARK - Set includes 30″ x 30″ vinyl playmat (not shown, says "Fisher-Price Amusement Park" along one side), combination tunnel/bridge/see-saw, flying chair ride, musical merry-go-round, single swing, four-piece train, two cars, two boats and seven figures. 1963-65. Original price - $7.99.

263 - #932 FERRY BOAT - 14″ x 9″ H. Large plastic ferry boat pull toy comes with two life preservers, speed boat, double passenger car, single passenger car and play family figures. 1979-80.

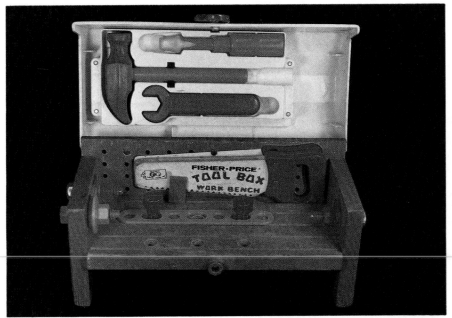

264 - #935 TOOL BOX WORKBENCH - 13″ x 6″ x 8¾″ H. Wooden bench has molded plastic hinged lid which holds screwdriver, hammer and wrench. Saw has plastic handle and paper litho on wooden blade. Vise not shown. Includes plastic nails, nuts, bolts and links. 1969-70. Courtesy of Tom Johnson.

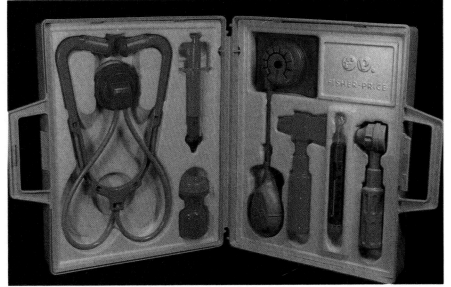

265 - #936 MEDICAL KIT - 10″ x 10″ x 3″. All plastic set includes case with white snap-in instrument trays, stethoscope, syringe, medicine bottle, blood pressure cuff, reflex hammer, thermometer and ear instrument. 1977-present.

266 - #937 SESAME STREET CLUBHOUSE - 17″ x 9⁷/₈″ x 9⁷/₈″ H. Set includes main piece with removable yellow slide, three snap-together barrels, one cable drum, jump rope mechanism, red wagon, and six figures: The Count, Roosevelt Franklin, Grover, Ernie, Bert and Big Bird. 1977-79.

267 - #938 PLAY FAMILY SESAME STREET - Set includes eight figures: Susan, Gordon, Mr. Hooper, Big Bird, Bert, Ernie, Cookie Monster, Oscar the Grouch in his can, Big Bird's nest, white ladder, T.V. set, couch, two beds marked "B" and "E", table and chairs, sanitation truck, light pole and sign, fire hydrant, mailbox, newsstand, and drugstore lunch counter. 1975-78.

268 - #939 - These are extra Sesame Street Characters available separately. Shown here are Mr. Snuffleupagus, Prairie Dawn, Herry Monster and Sherlock Hemlock. 1976-79.

269 - #942 LIFT 'N' LOAD DEPOT - 14¾″ x 6¼″ x 11¾″ H. Set includes main depot building, dump truck, scoop loader, fork lift, three workers, two pallets, two barrels, two gray crates and two tan crates. 1977-79.

270 - #945 OFFSHORE CARGO BASE - Twenty-two piece playset for water or floor includes: captain, two workers, deep sea diver, two sets of chains, six pieces of cargo, cargo net, helicopter, tugboat, barge, helicopter deck and cargo bin, crane base and covered cargo hold, docking location and cargo hold, and two rectangular black floats. 1979-83.

271 - #961 THE WOODSEY'S STORE - Set includes: fabric and vinyl hollow tree store, vinyl pushcart, chairs, potbellied stove, cloth ''basket'' holding fruits and vegetables, two finger puppets (Grandma and Grandpa Woodsey), and storybook *Grandma and Grandpa's Grand Opening.* 1980-82.

272 - #962 THE WOODSEY'S AIRPORT - Set includes: fabric over urethane foam airplane and hangar, Uncle Filbert Woodsey (pilot) finger puppet, and storybook, *Uncle Filbert Saves The Day.* 1980-82.

273 - #969 MUSIC BOX FERRIS WHEEL - 9¼″ x 6½″ base. Plastic and wood on fiberboard base. Includes four figures. Music box plays "In the Good Old Summertime." 1966-81.

274 - #972 CASH REGISTER - 8″ x 7″ x 8″ H. Wood, fiberboard and plastic. Came with wooden coins which fit into corresponding slots under keys. 1960-72. Price in 1963 - $3.57.

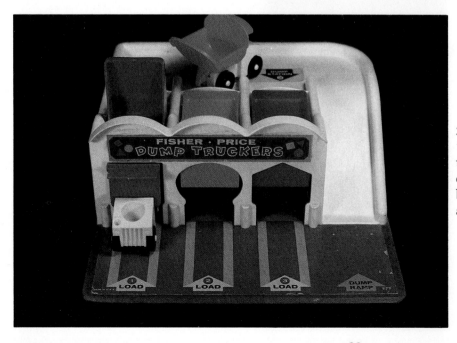

275 - #979 - DUMP TRUCKERS - 12⅝″ x 11⅝″ x 5″ H. Set includes: main piece, three plastic trucks whose color and shape correspond to truck loading bays, three black balls and three drivers. (Balls, drivers and one truck not shown.) 1965-70.

276 - #985 - PLAY FAMILY HOUSEBOAT - Set includes: houseboat, two life preservers, five figures (Captain, woman, girl, boy and dog), table showing lobster and plates with sailboat motif, two captain's chairs, BBQ grill, two deck loungers, and speedboat. 1972-present.

277 - #990 SAFETY SCHOOL BUS - 14¼″ x 5¾″ x 5¾″. Top of bus, "stop sign," driver's cap bill and hinge plates on door are plastic. Door opens. When pulled, driver's head turns side to side and bus "eyes" roll. Five older style figures included. 1962-65. Price in 1963 - $3.74.

278 - #990 PLAY FAMILY A-FRAME - Set includes: plastic A-frame cabin, two deck loungers, two sets of bunk beds, two chairs, ladder, picnic table and two benches, BBQ grill, jeep-type vehicle, and five family figures. 1975-76.

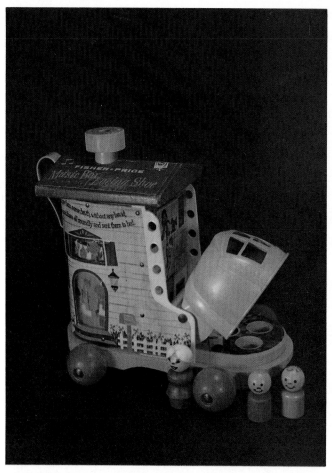

279 - #991 MUSIC BOX LACING SHOE - 8½″ x 8½″. Sole and roof are wooden, rest of shoe is in plastic and paper lithos. When chimney is wound, cylinder inside turns to show various scenes through the window. Comes with old woman and children figures. 1964-66.

281 - #993 PLAY FAMILY CASTLE - Castle is 17″ x 12¾″ x 13¼″ H. Set includes: main castle, carriage and harness, two horses, two thrones, two short chairs with crowns on the back, round table, double bed with crown, two single beds with crowns, knight and horse armor, woodsman, King, Queen, Prince and Princess, and a dragon. 1975-77.

280 - #991 CIRCUS TRAIN - Four piece train includes engine, lion cage, flatcar, and caboose. Vinyl hook and eye connectors. Animals, all vinyl and fully jointed, include giraffe, lion, elephant, monkey and bear. Play figures are clown, train engineer and ringmaster. 1973-80.

282 - #994 PLAY FAMILY CAMPER - Set includes: plastic pickup truck, lift-off cab-over camper, fishing boat, sink, commode, umbrella table, picnic table and four chairs, BBQ grill, trail bike and five family figures. 1972-76.

283 - #995 MUSIC BOX RECORD PLAYER - 9″ x 8½″ x 4¼″. All plastic record player has a wind up knob and an on/off switch. Comes with five numbered records which play two songs each. Various colors of plastic were used for records. 1971-present.

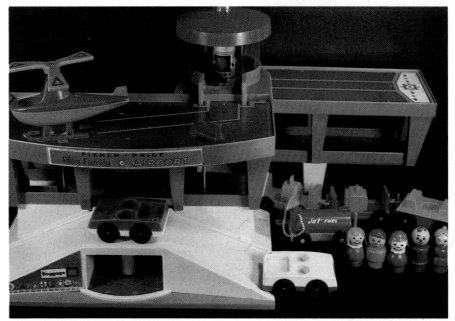

284 - #996 PLAY FAMILY AIRPORT - Closed size: 13¾″ x 13¾″ x 10¾″ H. Set includes: main airport building, helicopter, two cars, jet fuel car, utility vehicle with two baggage carriers, four-pieces luggage, stewardess, four piece play family, helicopter pilot (not shown) and the same airplane as the #183 Fun Jet with different paper lithos on tail. Also has turquoise plastic tail and wings instead of red. 1972-76.

285A and 285B - #997 PLAY FAMILY VILLAGE - 18″ x 12¾″ x 8½″ H. (closed size.) Set includes: two sections of village buildings, archway with traffic light, umbrella table and two chairs, BBQ grill and two chairs, barber chair, dentist chair, police car, mail truck, fire truck, car, mailman, policewoman, fireman, dentist (barber same as dentist), phone booth, color-coded plastic "letters" for each door slot, girl, boy, woman and dog. 1973-77. First photo: closed set. Second photo: open set.

286 - #997 MUSIC BOX TICK-TOCK CLOCK - 6½″ x 10½″ H. Plastic handle, hands, turning knobs and clock face. Music box plays and hands turn. 1962-67. Price in 1963 - $3.49. Courtesy of Betty Jane Updike.

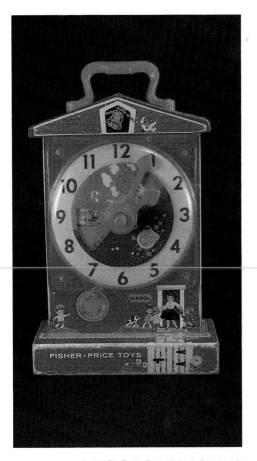

288 - #999 HUFFY PUFFY TRAIN - 27″ total length, 6½″ H. A few plastic parts include: the hook and eye connectors; piston rod; cowcatcher piece; sliding doors; and brakeman's hat, arms and lantern. The paint colors and lithos changed occasionally. Four piece train consists of engine, flatcar, box-car and caboose. 1958-69.

287 - #998 MUSIC BOX TEACHING CLOCK - 6½″ x 10½″ H. The same toy as #997 with different paper lithos. 1968-present.

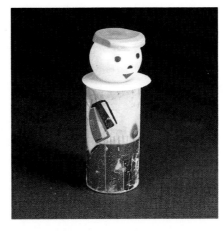

289 - This photo shows the earliest type Fisher-Price figure. This little boy was a part of the #983 Safety School Bus set made from 1959 to 1961. The body is paper litho over wood, the head is painted wood and the cap and collar are plastic. He is 2⁷/₈″ tall.

290 - This fireman has a painted wood body and head, plastic arms and hat. He is also 2⁷/₈″ tall, and he originally came with the #168 Snorky Fire Engine made in 1960 and 1961.

291 - Wooden people. While these figures do have plastic hair, hats or collars, both their bodies and heads are painted wood. The evolution continued when they came with plastic heads and wooden bodies. The same little folks made today are all plastic.

FULTON

292 - FULTON SIGN WRITER - Fulton Specialty Company box is 9⁷/₈″ x 4¼″. Set includes small individual pieces of rubber type which can be set into a wooden block for printing as well as individual letter and number stamps of wood and rubber. Also small metal pincers to pick up type.

FUN-E-FLEX

293 - FUN-E-FLEX MICKEY AND MINNIE MOUSE - 4″ H. Wooden figures have leather ears, arms, legs and tails. Mid-1930s. Courtesy of and photographed by Kathryn Fain.

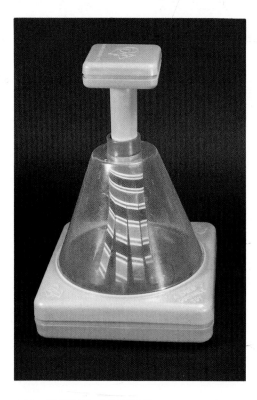

294 - POUND AROUND - 7½″ sq. base, 11″ H. When plunger is pushed down, red, white and blue swirl paper and multi-colored plastic balls whirl around inside clear plastic cone. 1978-present.

GABRIEL

Jerry Fryer and Morton Levy, both involved with the toy industry as manufacturers' representatives for 12 years, purchased a small toy company named Samuel Gabriel and Sons Co., Inc., in 1957. The two men changed the name of their company to Gabriel Industries, Inc., and continued to acquire more small toy and sporting goods firms for the next four years. In 1965, Hubley and Gym-Dandy both became part of Gabriel. They were joined in 1967 by the Erector & Science Lines of A. C. Gilbert, in 1973 by Kohner and in 1978 by the Child Guidance line, formerly part of Questor. In late 1978, CBS, Inc., acquired Gabriel Industries. Management of Creative Playthings and Wonder Toys, previously acquired by CBS, was assigned to Gabriel. The Gabriel name is being gradually phased out and will eventually be replaced by CBS, Inc.

295 - CONEY ISLAND ACTION ARCADE - 19″ L. x 8¼″ W. x 8″ H. Yellow and pink plastic back with paper lithos is attached to orange pressed wood base. Three vinyl figures (sideshow barker, girl and boy) play five miniature carnival games. c. 1978.

296 - WANNABEES FIRE ENGINE NO. 9 - 7″ L. x 5¼″ H. Red plastic fire engine with hose reel and two Wannabee firemen. 1975.

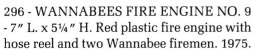

297 - WANNABEES FARMER, WIFE & HORSE - These three figures are part of a set which also included a farm wagon and harness for the horse. 1975.

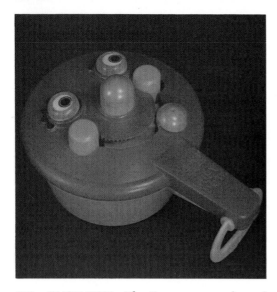

298 - BUSY POT - Plastic saucepan-shaped baby toy has mirror on the bottom and a face on top. Cheek buttons push in and out, nose squeaks, eyes roll when tongue is moved. Various colors. c. 1978.

300 - MECHANICAL MICKEY MOUSE - 9¼″ H. Molded plastic Mickey has see-through body to make working gears visible. He "walks" and swings his arms. c. 1978.

299 - BUSY BEEZER - Infant toy which attaches to crib side. Center button in flower beeps when pushed. Bird-shaped handle is attached to a cord which makes the bee fly upward, flapping its wings when it is pulled. c. 1978.

301 - BIG MOUTH SINGERS - Battery operated keyboard toy. When keys are depressed, the corresponding singer opens its mouth to "sing." 1978-present.

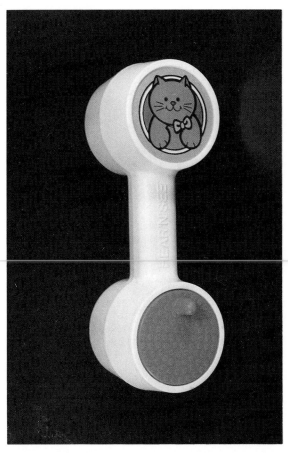

303 - COOKIE MONSTER PIANO - 9½″ H. When keys are played, black centers in Cookie's eyes twirl. All plastic with paper lithos. 1976-present.

302 - HEAR 'N' SEE - 7″ L. Dumbell-shaped infant toy. One end has mirror on one side, picture of cat on the other. The opposite end has a button squeaker and a rotating disc that clicks. Tilting toy back and forth makes mechanism inside "meow." c. 1978.

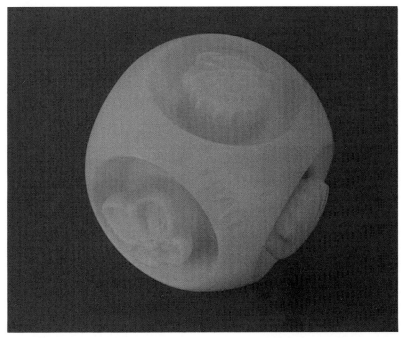

304 - BUSY CLUTCH BALL - Yellow vinyl ball has recessed areas facilitating grasping by infant.

305 - BUSY CLOCK - All plastic activity toy. Button on top squeaks, hands click when moved, and winding key in back makes bell ring.

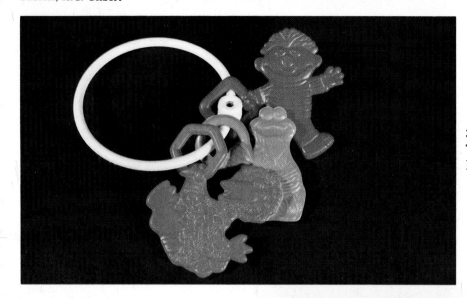

306 - MUPPETS SESAME STREET TEETHING RING - Big Bird, Cookie Monster, and Ernie on flexible vinyl ring.

A. C. GILBERT

Founded in 1909, this company is best known for its erector sets and chemistry sets. These lines were acquired by Gabriel Industries in 1967. The "Swinging Clowns" shown here exhibit their close kinship to the erector sets.

307 - SWINGING CLOWN - Metal litho clowns hang on each end of metal bar stand. Each one holds a small "jingle bell." When frame is rocked, clowns bob up and down and twirl over the bar. Date unknown.

308 - GILBERT "KIDDIKINS" - Red cylinder is $2^7/_8$" L. A wooden building set with many different pieces. Only these few were found with the instruction sheet. Package was a 10" jar. c. 1939. Price in 1939 - $1.00.

GILBERT TOYS
World Famous for 43 Years!

"I'M BOBBY GILBERT"

$1⁹⁵

GILBERT ANCHOR BLOCK SET — (For 2 and 3 year olds)
Here's a compact set with just the right number of Anchor Blocks and parts to enable smaller children to build interesting but not complicated models. Set has 24 Anchor Blocks, all properly weighted for piling, and includes whole and half sizes plus a chimney and four peak sections. Completing the set are a roof and illustrated Building Book. Box measures 10½ inches x 9 inches wide x 1¼ inches. Ask for 36BR1 (No. 2).
Other model larger and bigger.

All prices subject to change without notice. Some items slightly higher in some sections of the South and West.

$8⁷⁵

GILBERT MICROSCOPE SET
Microscope magnifies specimens 60, 90 and 210 TIMES ACTUAL SIZE. Lenses are precision ground optical glass. Focusing can be done quickly, sharply. With Polaroid attachment gorgeous colors come in view. Test tubes, forceps, dozen chemicals, slides, hand lens, etc., make complete laboratory. Set 18 inches x 10 inches x 2½ inches. By Gilbert. Ask for 36BR2. No. 8

GILBERT CHEMISTRY Senior Laboratory
Jam packed with enough chemicals and apparatus to perform 379 thrilling experiments! Three shelves of lightproof brown bottles, totaling 21 different kinds, plus 14 other chemicals provide ample material for home laboratory work. Alcohol lamp, glass stirring rods, funnel, etc., also included. Set has three huge books of fascinating experiments. Big, two-compartmented hinged chest stands 11½ inches high and opens to 20¼ inches width. Set folds to 9¾ inches wide x 11½ inches high x 2¾ inches deep. By Gilbert. Ask for 36BR4. No. 7

$9⁹⁵

GILBERT PUZZLE SET
There are nearly two-dozen twisters in this big Gilbert assortment including the puzzle of the Heathen Rings, the Conjuring Rings, the Twin Links, etc. Ideal for puzzle parties, rainy afternoons, auto trips, and other occasions. Illustrated booklet provides solutions. Set measures 18 inches long x 10 inches wide x 1¼ inches high. By Gilbert. Ask for 36BR3. No. 1032

$2⁰⁰

309Xa - Gilbert ad from 1952 *Billy & Ruth Catalog.*

ERECTOR — The Electric Engine Set

Has more than 350 parts, including Girders, Gears, Pinions, Wheels, Plates, Bolts, etc. Powerful Electric Engine gear train runs in forward and reverse, has multiple speed combinations. Set builds such models as the Lift Bridge, Windmill Pump, Airplane Beacon, Pile Driver; Delivery Truck, Hoist, Elevator and hundreds of others. Box is 18 inches long x 10 inches wide x 3 inches high. Big illustrated book. By Gilbert. Ask for 37BR1. No. 6½

12⁹⁵

Billy Likes **GILBERT** *World Famous* **ERECTOR SETS**

GILBERT TOOL CHEST — 12-Piece Set

Handsome all-steel hinged chest serves for real "on-the-job" work! Set comprises Screw Driver, 10 inch Saw, Mallet, Pliers Sanding Block, 6 inch metal Triangle Hammer, 45° Triangle, 12 inch T-Square Sandpaper supply, Plumb Bob, Utility Can. Chest measures 14½ inches x 8½ inches x 3 inches. By Gilbert. Ask for 37BR2. No. 5

5⁰⁰

JUNIOR ERECTOR

Wonderful for children in the 2 to 6 age group. Models are put together by fitting a hollow tube OVER a knob, rather than (in conventional construction sets) lining up and pushing tube INTO a hole. All parts finished in brilliant colors; children simply match up reds, greens, blues, etc. Set makes Beach Boat, Derrick, Trestle Bridge and dozens of other fascinating models. Box measures 20½ inches x 13¼ inches x 1¼ inch. By Gilbert. Ask for 37BR3. No. 4

3⁹⁵

7⁹⁵

ERECTOR-BRIK SET

Only the imagination of the youngster limits the number of DIFFERENT kinds of houses, forts, palaces, etc., which can be built with this Erector-Brik set. New exclusive material makes Briks wonderfully smooth and break-proof. Brilliant reds and marble whites. Set has 273 Briks and corrugated roof. All Briks have patented lock-together construction to build straight and true, with no toppling. Measures 20½ inches long x 13 inches wide x 1¼ inches high. By Gilbert. Ask for 37BR4. No. 2

309Xb - Gilbert ad from 1952 *Billy & Ruth Catalog.*

110

THE GONG BELL MANUFACTURING COMPANY

The Gong Bell Manufacturing Company was one of four bell companies in East Hampton, Connecticut during the late 1800s. The 1884 *History of Middlesex County, Connecticut*, states that the company was a "copartnership concern, composed of H. H. Abbe, A. H. Conklin, E. G. Cone and E. C. Barton. They commenced the manufacture of gongs and other varieties of bells in 1866 . . . some 5,000 gross of bell toys, besides large quantities of door, hand, table, call and sleigh bells are produced annually." They were the pioneers in 1872 in the manufacture of revolving chimes on wheels, and they control some 20 different patents. The Gong Bell Company produced toys until ceasing operations in 1960. (Information courtesy Marjorie Anderson, Director, East Hampton Public Library.)

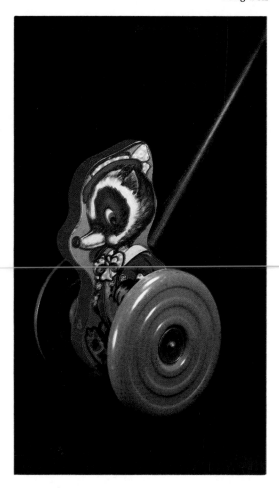

310 - FOX PUSH-ALONG - 9½" H., handle length 27½", wheel diameter 5¼". Fox is paper lithos on wood. Handle is wooden, wheels are painted metal and axle is wooden. Gong Bell's characteristic rolling "bells" are on each side of the fox. c. 1945.

311 - TUGBOAT SHOO-FLY - 81" L. x 12½" W. x 15½" H. Tugboat sides are painted wood. Painted wooden play tray, footrest and two-piece seat are attached to sides with screws. Plastic safety belt with metal buckle. Gong Bell's characteristic rocker-style bell used on their riding toys is under the seat. c. 1946.

312 - DOG CLOWN PULL TOY - 11" L. x 8" H. Dog is paper lithos over wood with a different picture on each side. Metal ring is supported by a metal frame which rolls on four red "bell" wheels. As toy is pulled, dog appears to do cartwheels. c. 1949.

313 - BLOCK WAGON - 15¼″ x 7⅞″ x 3⅝″. Paper lithos over wooden sides, pressed wood bottom, metal bell wheels.

314 - STROLLER CHIME - 10″ H. x 7¼″ W. Paper lithos on wooden seat, nickel plated armrests, enamelled metal "bell" wheels and an 18½″ long wooden push handle (handle not shown.) c. 1952. Price in 1952 - $1.49.

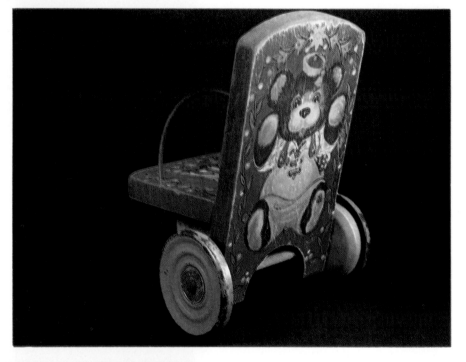

315 - VOICE PHONE - Metal desk-style phone. When dial is turned, striker vibrates between bells. This model came in red or blue. c. 1952. The price in 1952 was $1.69. Gong Bell made this toy with slight variations since at least 1930. Courtesy of Liz Robertson.

Hello Every-body!

Dial SANta 1-9-3-0 and hear his merry sleigh-bells jingle - with this really-truly Plaphone. It is a Gong Bell Toy - a wonderful value, beautifully finished. The dial turns and rings both ways. Look for Gong Bell Toys at the stores. Safe, durable, realistic and most for your money. If you don't find our Plaphone (they are selling so rapidly) mail us one dollar and it will come to you post paid.

$1.00

POST PAID IF NOT AT YOUR DEALER

No. 675

THE GONG BELL MFG. CO.
10 Walnut Ave., East Hampton, Conn.

316X - GONG BELL PLAPHONE ad from 1930 *Child Life* magazine. Courtesy of Bianca Hoekzema.

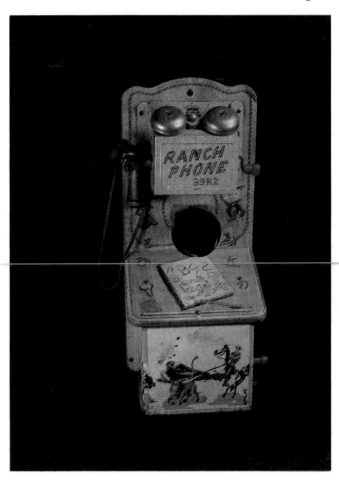

317 - RANCH PHONE - 13¼″ H. x 6″ W. x 4½″ Deep. Fiberboard back and slant desktop, metal mouthpiece, wooden receiver, green woven cotton cord, metal litho bell box and box base. Turning red plastic handle at top makes bells ring, turning the one at the bottom plays a concealed record message. c. 1952.

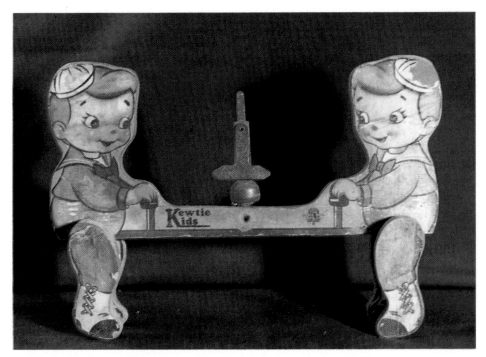

318 - KEWTIE KIDS - 12″ L. x 9″ H. This is the main piece of a see-saw toy. Some sort of stand fits through the center hole, and a bell fit on the center post so that the swinging hammer would ring it. c. 1943. Courtesy of and photo by Betty Jane Updike.

319 - KEWTIE KIDS "MISS AMERICA" - 9¾" L. x 4⅝" W. x 12-14" H. Paper lithos over wooden figure and lyre bell support, enamelled metal platform base, painted wooden wheels. As toy is pulled, arms move up and down and mallets strike bell. c. 1943.

320 - DOGGIE HAND CAR - 13¾" x 4¾" x 7" H. Painted metal platform has wooden wheels. Dogs are paper lithos over wood. Dog's "arms" move and alternately ring bell when toy is pulled.

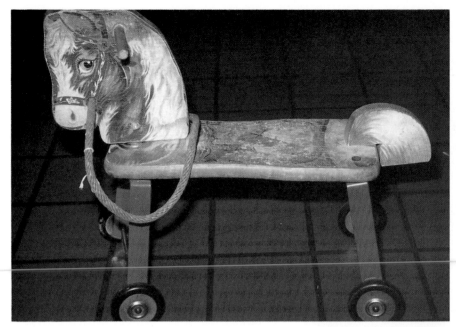

321 - RIDING HORSE - 21½″ L. x 18″ H. Paper lithos over wooden head, tail and seat. Metal "legs" and hard rubber wheels. Front wheels and head turn from side to side. Bell under seat. c. 1955.

322 - RIDING ZEBRA - 21½″ L. x 18″ H. Paper lithos over wooden head, tail and seat. Heavy cardboard tube legs fit over a steel frame and twirl barber-pole fashion as zebra moves along. Bell under seat rings. (Bridle replaced.) c. 1956. Price in 1956 - $3.49.

323 - SPECIAL DELIVERY SCOOTER - Paper lithos cover wooden box seat and body. Handlebars, bells, front bracket and wheels are metal. Tires are hard rubber. Hinged seat lifts up to load cargo. Courtesy of and photo by Betty Jane Updike.

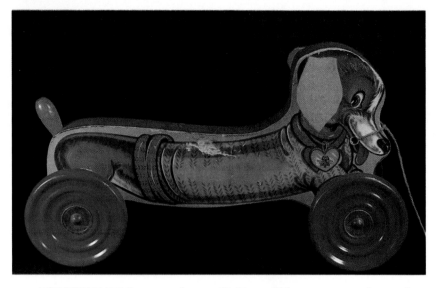

324 - DUTCHIE DOG - 11¼″ L. x 6″ H. Paper lithos over wood, wooden tail, felt ears and metal "bell" wheels. c. 1950.

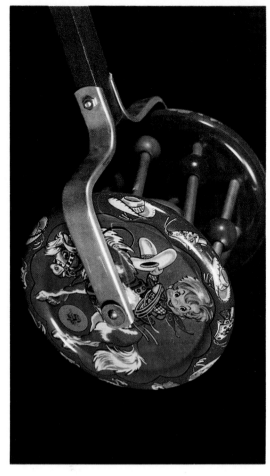

325 - MOWER CHIME - 8″ W. x 28″ H. overall. Wheels are lithographed metal, center chime and bracket is metal. Handle, axle, beads and the rods they slide on are all painted wood. c. 1950.

GONG BELL TOYS

Since 1866, Gong Bell toys have entertained American girls and boys because they have every requisite of good toys. Each is carefully and skillfully created to provide hours of play appeal through realistic action, colorful design and musical chimes. Gong Bell toys are educational, safe, and are quality constructed to withstand the hard use of eager users.

Sue says, "For little tots like me A Plaphone's just the thing, 'Cause I can turn the dial myself And hear my Plaphone ring."

0685 VOICE PHONE
Realistic, with shiny bells — Revolve the dial — bells ring. Lift the receiver — voice sounds. Spring return dial.

0683 DIAL PLAPHONE
Brightly enameled all steel. Revolve dial and hear shiny bells ring — realistic spring return dial.

VOICE VOICE

326X - Section from a Gong Bell advertisement featuring phones for tots.

THE HALSAM COMPANY

In 1917, Hal Elliot and Sam Goss returned from the army and World War I. Wanting to get into the toy business, they bought a small woodworking company in Michigan which specialized in making wooden blocks and moved it to Chicago. The new Halsam Company continued to produce wooden blocks and added checkers, dominos and construction sets to their products. The first Halsam plant was completely destroyed by fire in 1927. Elliot and Goss were down, but not out; they rebuilt their business in the same location. Due in part to the 1953 acquisition of The Embossing Company, a manufacturer of wooden blocks, checkers and dominos since 1870, the expanding company was moved to a larger and more modern plant. The Halsam Company was purchased by Playskool in 1962.

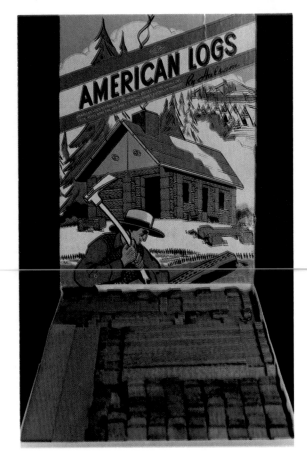

327 - AMERICAN LOGS - Building sets, similar to the more familiar "Lincoln Logs," came in several sizes.

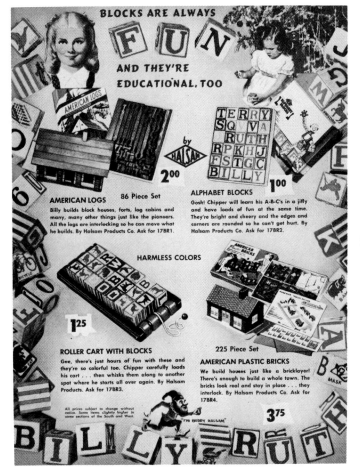

328X - Page 16 of the *Billy & Ruth 1952 Catalog*

HASBRO INDUSTRIES, INC.

329 - MR. POTATO HEAD - This toy was introduced in 1948. At that time, the plastic pieces were meant to be stuck into a real potato to create a figure. A plastic potato was added to the set in 1952. The set pictured here was introduced in 1964, and it was called "Mr. Potato Head and His Tooty-Frooty Friends." Not all of the pieces in the set are shown, only a representative sampling. Suggested retail in 1964 was $2.00. In 1968, the line was expanded to include not only the spring-wound "Jumpin' Mr. and Mrs. Potato Head," but also 30-piece sets called "Frankie Frank," "Frenchy Fry," and "Willy Burger." In 1969 Mr. Potato Head went on seven new adventures. These included appropriate pieces for "Mr. Potato Head On The Moon," ". . . On The Railroad," ". . . In The Parade" and ". . . On The Farm." The three larger playsets, "Wild West," "Masquerade" and "Circus" had over 80 pieces, including a background scene. In 1970, Mr. Potato Head was joined in one set by Donald Duck and in another by Bozo the Clown.

331 - "POPEYE" GUM MACHINE BANK - All plastic with a glued-on paper eye. c. 1968-75.

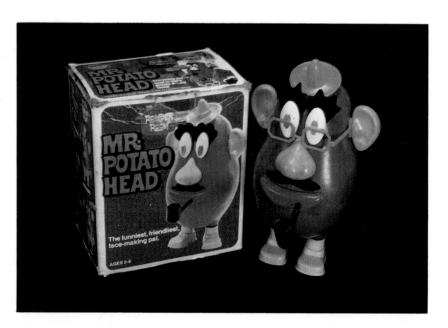

330 - MR. POTATO HEAD - By 1965, Mr. Potato Head looked like this. Additional accessories were available to create a fireman, a woman and a sheriff.

332 - DANCING DONALD - 18" H. Foam-stuffed figure on wire armature had vinyl head and hands. Squeezing hands makes legs move back and forth to "dance." Marching Mickey (Mickey Mouse) was also available. c. 1977.

333 - WEEBLES TUMBLIN' FUNHOUSE - Weighted Weebles tumble end over end from one level of the house to another. Playset includes: main house with winding elevator, two weighted Weebles, car, three sections of track and tree.

334A and 334B - WEEBLES HAUNTED HOUSE - Main house is hinged in the center to open and close. Wall of books in library revolves to show mirror on opposite side. Play pieces include: couch, chair, bed, trunk with bats in lid, Ghost Weeble which glows in the dark, Witch Weeble and hat, Girl Weeble and Boy Weeble. c. 1976.

335 - WEEBLES GHOST VAN - 6" L. x 4" H. Lavender plastic delivery van with black plastic wheels. Window on opposite side has bars. Pressing bars inward opens back door. Ghost Weeble and labels on van glow in dark. c. 1977.

336 - WEEBLES TREASURE ISLAND - Playset includes: pirate ship with removable sails, flag and hatch cover, pirate captain with removable hat, three pirate "mates," two islands, three palm trees, one with lookout platform, hammock, hut, long boat, pick and shovel, treasure chest, three piers, (pirate treasure map, one pirate Weeble and one hat missing from photo.) c. 1975.

337 - WEEBLES WIGWAM - Four-piece playset includes: 6" T. white plastic tepee with orange top stakes, orange travois, white horse with saddle and Indian Weeble. c. 1975.

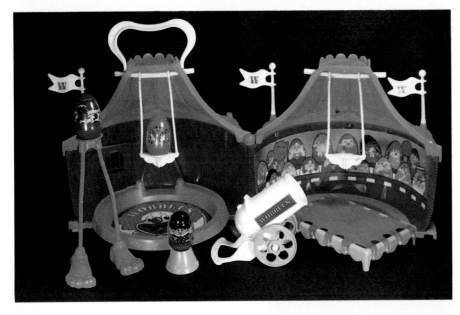

338A and 338B - WEEBLES CIRCUS - 8¾″ x 9¾″ x 9⁷/₈″ H. (main piece.) Plastic tent is also a carrying case. Two white trapezes are attached inside the "big top." Play pieces include: cannon; trampoline; stilts on big feet; tub; trapeze artist, Gina Weeble; clown, Wobbles Weeble; ringmaster, Bart Weeble; four white "W" flags which fit on tent; (red hoop that fits on trampoline and one flag missing from photo.) c. 1977. Price in 1977 - $7.94.

339 - SUPER WEEBLE HERO - Weebles are 2″ H. Set contains ice cream truck (same as Ghost Van, but a different color,) office trailer and two Weebles. One is "Mr. Trouble," and the other can be changed from "mild-mannered Walter Weeble" to "Super Weeble!" by turning the center. c. 1977.

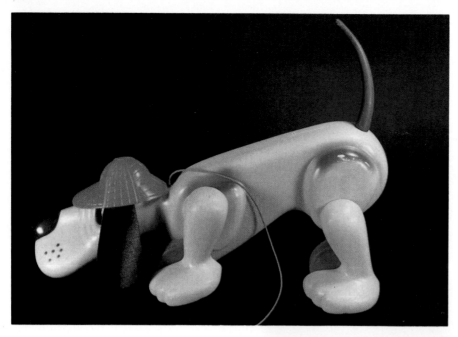

340 - DIGGER THE DOG - 13¾″ L. x 9½″ H. All plastic with vinyl tail and ears. Pulling the leash-string makes Digger run across the floor. c. 1974-80.

341 - LITTLE DIGGER THE DOG - 7½″ L. This is a friction toy version of the big Digger.

342 - RICOCHET RACERS - Launcher is 21″ long. Cars in cases are 4¼″-4½″. Metal cars in plastic cases are inserted cartridge-fashion into the launcher. Cars race across the floor when trigger is pulled. c. 1974.

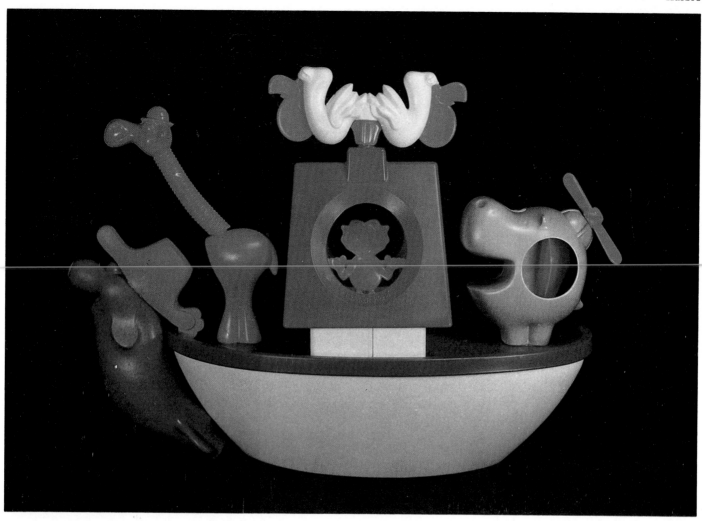

343 - SQUIRT, SQUIRT THE ANIMALS - Boat: 12″ L. x 9¼″ H. (10½″ with pelicans.) This is a water target game toy and is all plastic or vinyl. Dolphin on the bow is a water pistol. He is squeezed to shoot at the moving parts of the various animals on board. c. 1978-present.

344 - SCOOTER THE TOOTER - All plastic clown has flexible vinyl arms. Pushing down on the bluebird makes Scooter blow a note. Turning the bird from side to side changes the note as the pipe slides the same direction. c. 1980-present.

HOLGATE TOYS

This company had its beginning in 1879 when Cornelius Holgate established a wood-working company in Philadelphia which produced items such as brushes and broom handles. The treasurer of Holgate had a daughter who married an educator and child psychologist named Lawrence Frank. Through his influence, the company began producing wooden toys in the early 1930s. Jerry Rockwell, brother of artist Norman Rockwell, was hired to design the toys. Because Rockwell was a brilliant and practical toy designer, many of the toys present in the 1932 line are still available today in slightly altered form. When Holgate merged with Playskool in 1958, Jerry Rockwell joined the Playskool staff and continued to design toys (such as his "Playskool Tyke Bike") until his retirement in 1971.

345 and 346 - STACKING RINGS - 9″ H. x 3″ Dia. at base. Twelve graduated wooden rings, making two complete color spectrums, fit onto a wooden post. The bottom red ring screws onto the threaded post to hold the others on. c. 1945.

347 - TASKET BASKET - 9″ L. x 6″ W. x 7″ H. Pentagonal basket is a shape sorter made of masonite-like material with two wooden ends and carrying handle. c. 1953.

348 - OCEAN LINER - 11″ L. x 4″ H. Wooden pull toy has painted wooden cylinders that fit into holes in top of the boat. Two wooden rings fit over the cylinders. Side design is painted on. c. 1950.

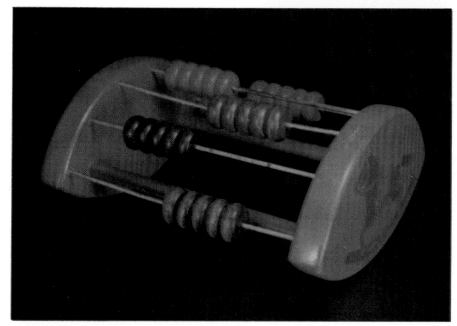

349 - ROCKING HORSE ABACUS - 8½″ L. x 7″ W. x 4″ H. Five wooden beads in each of six rainbow colors are held by five metal rods inserted into irregular oval ends made of maple wood. Two wooden rods add support.

350A and 350B - TAKE-APART COLDSTREAM GUARD - 17½″ H. Separate pieces include square wooden base, hat, head, collar, arms and hands, and legs cylinder. The body is a cardboard cylinder with a wooden disc on each end. c. 1947.

351 - WOODEN LACING SHOE - 10″ L. x 4″ H. Natural wood shoe has blue tongue, green toe and sole. Shoe has round hole in back of heel into which to fit "Old Woman" and her children. Woman and children are painted, turned wooden figures. c. 1940s.

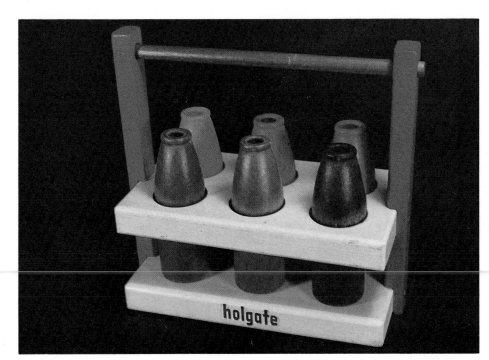

352 - MILK BOTTLES AND CARRIER - 8″ L. x 4″ W. x 7½″ H. All wooden carrier holds six wooden bottles in color spectrum order: red, orange, yellow, green, blue, violet.

353 - TEACH-A-TOT DAIRIES - Bottles are 3¼″ H. Six wooden milk bottles in a cardboard holder.

HUSTLER TOYS

354 - HUSTLER PUP - Base: 6¼″ L. x 2¾″ W.; 8″ H. overall. Wooden bulldog once had cloth ears and glued-on burgundy collar with gold markings. Dog is mounted on metal litho base which rolls on wooden wheels. Mechanism under platform moves dog's legs individually, making him walk. The same toy may bear the "FRANTZ MFG. CO." mark instead of the Hustler trademark. 1930s.

355 - JOE HUSTLER TRANSFER - 10½″ L. x 3¾″ W. x 5¼″ H. Metal litho base with wooden wheels carries wooden cargo box and turned wooden man who moves back and forth when toy is pulled. Trademark on this toy reads: "Frantz Mfg. Co./The Hustler Family." 1930s.

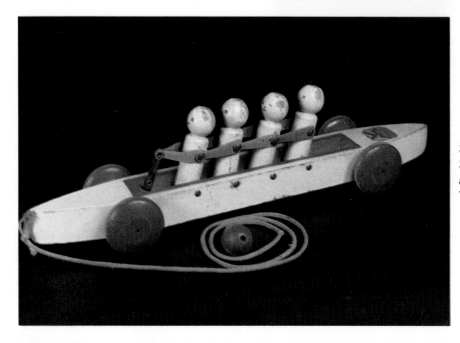

356 - ROWING TEAM - 14″ L. x 3″ W. x 3¾″ H. Turned wooden figures with metal arms row in unison as toy is pulled. Wooden boat and wheels. 1930s.

357 - PINOCCHIO - 10½″ H. Jointed figure of painted wood. c. 1940s. Courtesy of and photographed by Kathryn Fain.

"IT'S A WONDERFUL TOY . . . IT'S IDEAL"

The Ideal Novelty and Toy Company was begun in 1907 by Mr. and Mrs. Morris Michtom.. Four years earlier, the Michtoms had owned and operated a stationery and novelty store. It was during that time that President Theodore Roosevelt had made his famous refusal to shoot a bear cub. Mrs. Michtom made a couple of "Teddy's Bears" by hand for the window of their store, and soon the demand for more of them made the new company a necessity. Ideal's best known successes have been in the doll line, but they have also made a great many familiar toys.

358 - PECKING CHICKEN - 4½″ L. x 3½″ W. x 5″ H. Red brittle plastic chicken "pecks" food from a white pan on yellow platform as toy is pulled. White plastic wheels and fence. c. 1950.

359 - DELIVERY VAN - 5″ L. x 2¼″ H. Brittle plastic van in yellow and green has red back doors which swing open and red sliding side doors. Rubber wheels are marked "Ideal." c. 1950.

360 - ROADSTER - 9″ L. x 3″ H. Red brittle plastic roadster has working steering wheel which turns front wheels. The "bonnet" raises on both sides. c. 1950.

361 - SCOOP LOADER - 8″ x 2¼″ x 4″ H. Brittle plastic truck with working scoop has rubber tires. Early 1950s.

362 - CARPET SWEEPER - 2″ x 1¾″ x 4½″ H. Brittle plastic sweeper has roller underneath. (Dust bag missing.) Early 1950s.

363 - FIX-IT TRUCK - 8″ L. x 4″ W. x 3½″ H. Brittle plastic truck has removable plastic wheels. Spare tire is in compartment under truck bed. Tools in tool box include lift-jack, screwdriver, wrench and hammer. c. 1951. Price in 1951 - $1.19.

364 - ROY ROGERS' FIX-IT STAGE-COACH - Overall length 15″. Coach height 6¼″. Molded brown plastic stagecoach has removable wheels held on-to axles by threaded metal nuts. Metal wrench included to change wheels. Gray plastic horses have vinyl harness. Dark gray plastic tool box and gold strongbox. Tools include: mallet, two-piece jack, jack handle, pry bar and two wheel wedges. Vinyl driver has whip and rifle. c. 1955.

366 - MECHANICAL DISHWASHER - 3½″ x 3¼″ x 5″ H. All plastic wind-up dishwasher has drain hose, lift-out basket, and plastic dishes. c. 1950.

365 - ROBERT, THE ROBOT - 13½″ x 7½″ x 6½″. Plastic robot has plastic hand control. Robot "walks" by turning cable handle. On/off knob on chest controls bulb on head (not shown here.) turning crank on back ac-tivates talking mechanism. Mid-1950s.

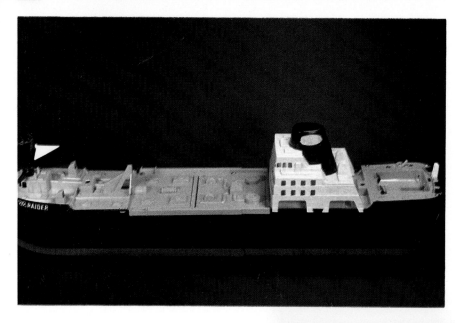

367A - PHANTOM RAIDER - Length closed, 28½"; open, 34". Battery-operated plastic ship. Control lever moves ship forward and backward, opens and closes weaponry hatches. Ship imitates ocean roll as it moves along on three wheels.

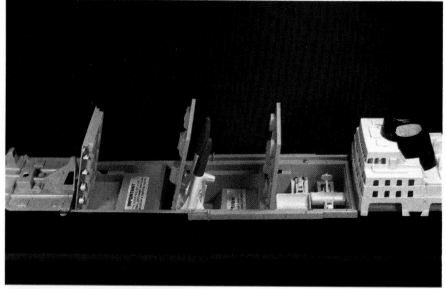

367B - PHANTOM RAIDER - Close up view. Weapons include: four torpedoes, two rockets and two depth charges. (Rear deck missing in photo.) c. 1964.

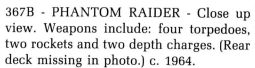

368 - "SUPER CITY" HELIPORT SET - This building set is one of several in the "Super City" series and stores in a "play 'n' carry" case. Components too numerous and varied to list individually include an opening garage door, bay window, store fronts, flagpole, awnings, doorways, etc. c. 1968.

369A and 369B - "SUPER CITY" SKYSCRAPER BUILDING SET - Similar to the Heliport set, this one contains over 350 pieces, including a helicopter. Other sets in this series were: 130-piece Basic Building Set, 200-piece Town and Country Set, 475-piece Skyport Set, Landscape Set and Roadway Accessory Set. All of these were designed to go with the "Motorific" line of cars and road race toys. c. 1968.

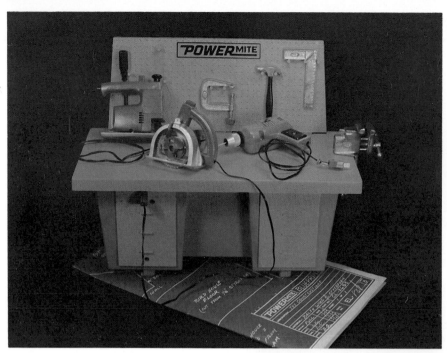

370 - POWERMITE WORKBENCH - 11″ x 5″ x 4¾″ H. Miniature workbench holds two "D" batteries which power a working metal drill, circle saw and sabre saw. Miniature hand tools - screwdriver, hammer, adjustable wrench and square - fit on separate tool board at the back. Vise clamps onto the side. All pieces fit inside workbench when not in use. c. 1969. Courtesy of Claude James.

371 - QUICKFLIP VOLLEYBALL - 17¼″ x 12″ H. Two sponge foam figures inside clear plastic face are controlled by front knobs to throw ball back and forth over the "net." Two blue plastic stands included. c. 1973.

372 - LIVE-IN TRAIN - Main live-in car: 15″ L. x 5″ H. Playset includes: three-piece plastic train, step unit, pot bellied stove, rocking horse, two benches and a table, a chair, blue barrel, two blue suitcases with metal circles on the sides, wrench and shovel, car, and the Mac Magnet Family, consisting of man, woman, girl, boy and dog. Figures have magnets in their hands to "pick up" tools and suitcases or to hold hands. (Missing are the barrel, tools, boy, girl and dog.) c. 1975.

373 - MR. MACHINE - 17½″ H. x 6″ W. A more recent version of the one introduced in 1960. This windup toy has a clear plastic body and large wheels. Actions include: rolling forward, swinging arms, opening and closing mouth, turning gears, and a bellows-operated "whistling tune." c. 1977.

374 - STAR HAWK - 13″ base diameter, 8″ H. The "Star Team" spaceship comes with Zeroid, a 5½″ gray, red and clear plastic robot with a battery-operated light and rubber treads. When latch is released on spaceship, hatch slides open, pads go into position, exit ramp lowers, and "boing-boing" sounds are made. Plastic ship has paper decals. c. 1977.

375 - "MR. ROGERS" NEIGHBORHOOD HAND PUPPETS - 13″ H. Stuffed cloth bodies have hollow vinyl heads. Shown here: King Friday, Lady Elaine and Owl. c. 1977.

376 - TEA SET - Teapot is 3″ H. Red marbled brittle plastic dishes. c. 1950.

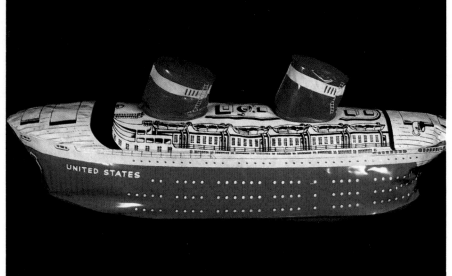

377 - UNITED STATES SHIP - 24″ x 6″ x 8″ H. This inflatable vinyl toy has flat cardboard bottom. Squeakers in smokestacks. c. 1950.

IRWIN

378 - IRWIN PROJECTOR - 5″ L. x 3¼″ H. All steel with baked-on black enamel. Operates on two "D" batteries. Celluloid film strip is advanced by turning crank handle, which can be removed for storage. Irwin films, which sold for 10¢, were issued in a comic series of Popeye, Koko, Buck Rogers, Betty Boop, Bimbo, Felix the Cat, Krazy Kat, and Scrappy. A train series included "Speed" and "Zephyr." c. 1930. Childhood toy of Margaret Mandel. Photo by Margaret Mandel.

KENNER

Kenner Products was formed in 1947 in Cincinnati, Ohio, by Al, Phil and Joe Steiner. The company took its name from its location on Kenner Street. Kenner's first toy was the "Bubble-Gun" in 1947. This was followed in 1949 by the "Bubble Rocket." Their "Six Million Dollar Man" line was tremendously successful in the mid-1970s; but Kenner's most spectacular success is the "Star Wars" line of toys, which came on the market in early 1978. According to Dale Pollock, author of "Skywalking; the Life and Films of George Lucas," if Kenner sold nothing but "Star Wars" merchandise, it would be the fifth largest toy company in the world.

379 - STORYTIME JUKEBOX - 12¼" x 7½" x 8" H. Battery operated jukebox uses a two-section cylindrical plastic record. All plastic. c. 1972. Price in 1972 - $16.99.

380 - GIVE-A-SHOW PROJECTOR - 9½" x 6" H. Battery operated brittle plastic projector shows film strips especially made for it. 1970s-present.

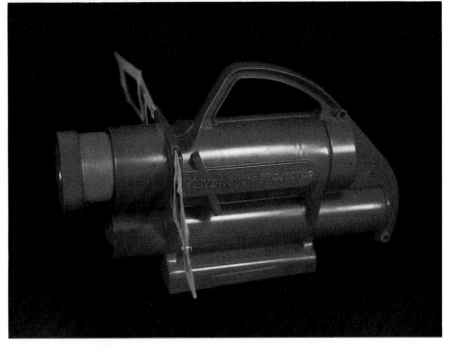

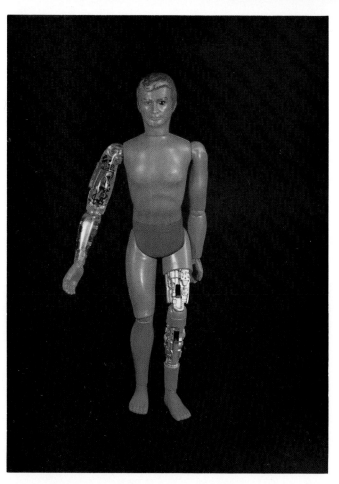

381 - SIX MILLION DOLLAR MAN ACTION FIGURE - 13″ H. fully jointed vinyl action figure has "bionic arm." This arm has "roll back" latex skin for replacing bionic components. c. 1975. Price in 1975 - $6.84.

382 - CRITICAL ASSIGNMENT ARMS SET - This photo shows the "neutralizer arm." Also included were a "laser arm" that shot a red beam of light and an "oxygen supply arm" and mask needed for high altitude missions. White T-shirt with Six Million Dollar Man logo included in set. c. 1976. Price in 1976 - $5.66.

383 - BIONIC MISSION VEHICLE - 20″ L. Plastic vehicle travels on three wheels. (Transparent shield, winch and cargo not shown.) c. 1977. Price in 1977 - $11.66.

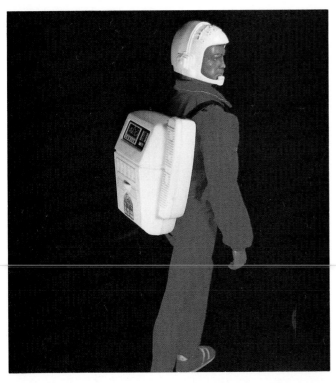

384 - SIX MILLION DOLLAR MAN BACKPACK RADIO - Plastic backpack holds ear plug and alligator clip. Radio signals are picked up by adjusting antenna when clip is grounded. Includes plastic helmet for Steve Austin. c. 1976. Price in 1976 - $4.95.

385 - SIX MILLION DOLLAR MAN COMMAND CONSOLE - Overall height, 14½″. Accessory playset includes: octagonal vinyl playmat, plastic and cardboard console center, plastic swivel chair, plastic binoculars and code transmitter, vinyl cables with plastic connectors. c. 1976.

386 - BIONIC TRANSPORT AND REPAIR STATION - 17½″ H. Combination rocket, bionic repair station and carrying case for action figure. The set includes: 2X microscope, "x-ray" unit, bionic control panel cables, revolving "radar" cone, revitalization chamber and read-out computer. c. 1975. Price in 1975 - $8.74.

387 - MASKATRON, SIX MILLION DOLLAR MAN'S ENEMY ACTION FIGURE - 13″ H. Fully jointed action figure whose head, forearms and lower legs pop off. Includes three snap-on faces, two snap-on weapon arms, shirt, pants and shoes. c. 1976. Price in 1976 - $7.44.

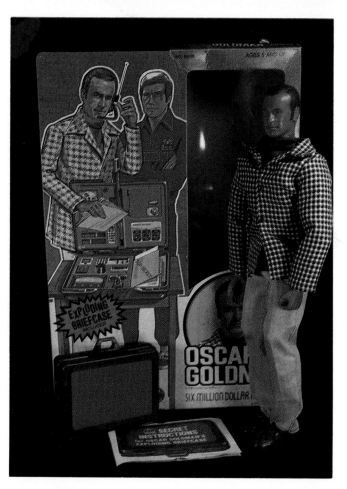

388 - THE BIONIC WOMAN - 12″ H. Fully jointed action figure has modules in right arm and both legs. c. 1976. Price in 1976 - $7.94.

389 - OSCAR GOLDMAN AND HIS EXPLODING BRIEFCASE - 13″ H. Fully jointed vinyl figure comes with shirt, pants, jacket, shoes and trick "exploding" briefcase. c. 1977. Price in 1977 - $7.44.

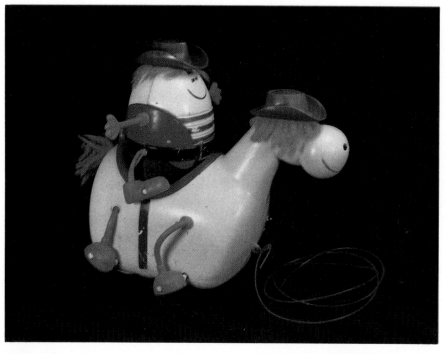

390 - GOOFY GUY AND GOOFY WALKER - 8″ L. x 4½″ W. x 7½″ H. Separate horse and rider are plastic with vinyl arms, legs and hats and yarn hair. c. 1975.

391A and 391B - TREE TOTS' HOUSE - Closed: 11″ H. x 11″ W.; open: 14″ H. Large plastic tree opens to reveal three-room house inside. Set includes: five Tree Tot figures: mother, father, girl, boy and dog; "bush" dog house; two beds and one couch; table and five chairs; and car. c. 1975. (Other sets available included: Tree Tots' Lighthouse, Tree Tots' Sky Coaster, Tree Tots' Amusement Park, and Tree Tots' Firehouse Tree.)

392 - STRETCH ARMSTRONG - 13″ H. figure with rubbery skin is filled with a semi-liquid substance and can be stretched to nearly four feet in length. Comes with 4′ vinyl "stretch-o-graph." c. 1976.

393 - GIRDER & PANEL INTERNATIONAL AIRPORT - A 325-piece set. One of several in this line of building sets. All plastic pieces with paper signs. c. 1977.

394 - MILKY THE MARVELOUS MILKING COW - 14½″ x 10½″ H. Molded plastic cow has vinyl hooves and udder and metal cow bell. Special coloring tablets are inserted into udder mechanism, which is then attached. Head is pushed down into watering trough. When tail is pumped, Milky "drinks" until she is full, then raises her head and "moos." Set includes: vinyl playmat and plastic trough, "milk" tablets, clear plastic milk pail, and booklet, "How We Get Milk."

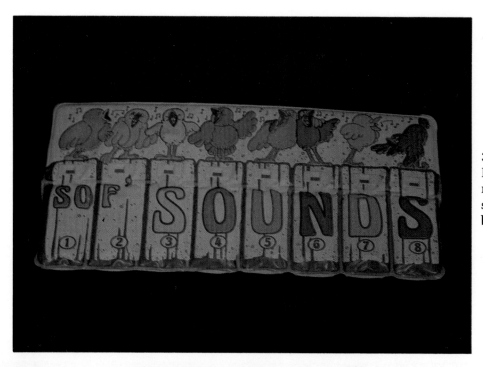

395 - SOF' SOUNDS - 17″ x 7½″. Foam-stuffed vinyl "pillow" plays musical scale when each numbered section is squeezed. Comes with song book. c. 1979.

396 - SEA WEES - Vinyl mermaids with rooted hair come with foam island and comb. c. 1980-present.

397 - SEA WEES LAGOON - Set contains: molded plastic island, vinyl blowfish for shower, plastic dressing table shell, four pieces of orange sponge coral and weighted plastic seahorse with beaded blue harness. (Harness not shown.) c. 1978.

398 - SEA WEES CASE - Molded plastic shell has divided interior to hold Sea Wees figures and accessories. c. 1980.

399 - STAR WAR BOOKETS - Included in the package with larger toys, these serve as reference guides to the collector. (First booklet dated 1977 did not actually come onto the market until 1978.)

400A and 400B - THE FIRST TWELVE ACTION FIGURES - These are the small (4″ or less) vinyl and plastic figures with appropriate accessories. 1978-present. First photo: Stormtrooper, Ben (Obi-Wan) Kenobi, C3PO, R2D2, Sandpeople (Tusken Raider), and Death Star Commander. (Style changes were made in both C3PO and R2D2 in 1982. C3PO's arms and legs became removable and R2D2 received a moving "Sensorscope.") Second photo: Chewbacca, Han Solo, Luke Skywalker, Princess Leia Organa, Jawa and Darth Vader.

401 - First 12 figures shown on the "Action Collectors" stand. Stand is 20″ L. x 6¼″ H. Plastic base with cardboard background insert. Not available on the retail level, this toy was a mail-in offer which expired May 1, 1979, and required $2.00 plus two proofs of purchase from action figure packages, or 12 proofs of purchase.

402 - LUKE SKYWALKER - 12″ H. Vinyl figure jointed at hips, shoulders and neck. Knees bend. Clothing includes: white vinyl boots, tan pants, white lap front shirt and black utility belt with grappling hook. (Green light saber not shown.) 1978-80.

403 - CHEWBACCA - 15″ H. Molded plastic "Wookiee" jointed at hips and shoulders. Accessories include: vinyl crossbow laser rifle, vinyl ammunition belt and pouch and 16 gray plastic snap-on ammunition cartridges. 1978-80.

404 - PRINCESS LEIA ORGANA - 11½″ Vinyl figure jointed at hips, shoulders and neck. Knees bend. Clothing and accessories include: white vinyl shoes, white tights, white gown and metallic belt, comb and brush for hair styling. 1978-80. Courtesy of Betty Jane Updike.

405 - DARTH VADER - 15″ Molded plastic figure jointed at hips, shoulders and neck. Synthetic fiber black cape. (Red light saber missing from photo.) 1978-80.

406A - DEATH STAR SPACE STATION - 22½″ H. x 16″ x 13″. (This photo of the original box also shows many of the small action figures.) Molded plastic "play environment" has manual elevator in dark gray central shaft. Swivelling laser cannon on top floor "explodes" when hit. Second floor has manually operated extending light bridge and hanging "escape rope." First floor is the control area and has escape hatch into the trash compactor below. Trash compactor has moving wall to crush foam "garbage" and a green vinyl monster. Two printed cardboard panels slide into exterior tracks. 1978-80.

406B - TRASH COMPACTOR MONSTER - 4½″ x 2¾″ x 1¼″ H. A closer view of the creature in the trash compactor. Courtesy Jason Franklin.

407 - ESCAPE FROM DEATH STAR BOARD GAME - Includes: gameboard, eight "playing tokens" (cards showing characters from movie on plastic bases), four Death Star blueprint cards, four Tractor Beam cards, spinner, and a deck of Force cards. 1978-79.

408 - X-WING ACES TARGET GAME - 23″ x 14¾″ x 1½″ H. Molded gray plastic body, black front and blue gun. Light images of T.I.E. fighters fly across recessed screen and explode when hit. Includes transformer. 1978.

409 - LAND SPEEDER - 9½″ x 6″ x 2¾″ H. Molded plastic vehicle with clear windshield. Button on front opens hood, shift lever lowers wheels. 1978-80. (Collector's Edition available in 1984.) Slightly larger remote-controlled Land Speeder with same hand control as "Jawa Sandcrawler" also available in 1979.

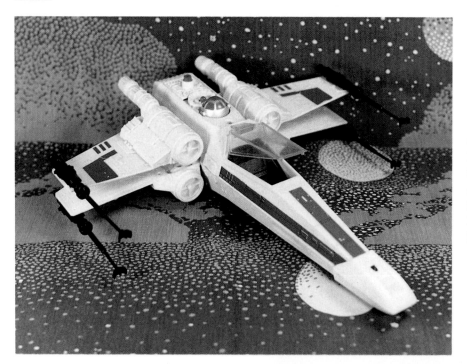

410 - X-WING FIGHTER - 13½″ x 12″. Molded plastic X-wing has battery operated laser gun light and sound, opening cockpit, and retractable landing skid. Pulling back release button and pushing down R2D2's head opens wings to "X" configuration. 1978-present.

411 - T.I.E. (TWIN ION ENGINE) FIGHTER - 10½″ x 9″ x 7″. Molded plastic T.I.E. Fighter has pop-off solar panels to simulate battle damage. Cockpit seat raises and lowers and hatch opens. Batteries operate laser cannon light and laser sound when rear deck button is pushed. 1978-81. (Collector's Edition available in 1984.)

412 - DIECAST LAND SPEEDER - 4¾″ x 3″ x 1³/₈″ H. Miniature metal model of the larger vehicle. (Windshield missing from photo.) 1978-81.

413 - DIECAST X-WING FIGHTER - 4¾″ x 4″ x 1½″ H. (wings open.) Cast metal body has plastic wings and hatch cover. 1978-81. Courtesy Jason Franklin.

414 - INFLATABLE LIGHT SABER - 35″ L. inflated. Inflatable vinyl tube fits on flashlight-type handle with "Star Wars" emblem around outside. Came with vinyl patch kit. This style produced 1978-80.

415 - LASER PISTOL - Plastic replica of Han Solo's laser pistol. "Star Wars" logo on side. 1978-83.

416 - THREE POSITION LASER RIFLE - 18½" L. Battery-operated molded plastic rifle has three-position stock. This example, marked 1978, is actually from 1980 due to bearing "Empire" logo rather than "Star Wars." "Star Wars" logo: 1978-79; "Empire", 1980-81.

417 - RADIO CONTROLLED R2D2 - 8" H. Battery-operated plastic robot and control. Head turns 360°, red "eye" lights up, electronic beeping sounds, and he moves in four different directions. 1978-80.

418 - "STAR WARS" MOVIE VIEWER - 6¾" x 6¾". Molded plastic viewer has handle and "Star Wars" logo on one side. Snap-in cartridge of scenes from the movie. 1978-79.

419 - R2D2 BOP BAG - 33" H. inflated. Inflatable vinyl punching bag is weighted in the bottom. 1978-79.

421 - CHEWBACCA PLUSH AND R2D2 PLUSH - Synthetic fur Chewbacca is 20″ tall, has plastic eyes and nose, and fabric mouth. (Bandolier strap missing from photo.) R2D2 is 10″ tall, has movable legs and "squeaks" when red spot is pressed. 1978-79.

420 - DARTH VADER BOP BAG - 45″ H. inflated. Inflatable vinyl punching bag is weighted in the bottom. 1978-79.

422 - "STAR WARS" PLAY-DOH ACTION SET - Includes: plastic modified X-Wing Fighter, three hinged molds, 10″ x 16″ platmat, trim knife and three 6-oz. cans of Play-Doh. 1978-79.

423 - 140-PC. JIGSAW PUZZLES - Two of the original four puzzles. 1978.

424 - 500-PC. JIGSAW PUZZLES - Two of the original four puzzles. 1978.

425 - JIGSAW PUZZLES - 500-Pc. Series III "Victory Celebration" and 140-pc. Series IV "Jawas Capture R2D2." 1978.

426 - "STAR WARS" SSP VANS - 7¼" L. x 3" W. x 3" H. Van exterior is all plastic, as is the T-stick. Center flywheel makes "Sonic Sound" and "Blazin' Sparks" when T-stick is pulled. A black "Darth Vader" van was also available. 1978-79.

427A and 427B - NEXT NINE ACTION FIGURES - These are vinyl figures, approximately 4" tall. First photo: Snaggletooth, Boba Fett, Hammerhead, Greedo and Walrusman. (The first Boba Fetts had firing rocket backpacks.) Second photo: Power Droid, Luke Skywalker in the X-Wing Pilot Outfit, Death Star Droid, and R5D4. 1979-present.

428 - ACTION FIGURES COLLECTOR'S CASE - 12″ x 8¾″ x 3″. Vinyl carrying case has snap shut lid and two removable plastic trays to hold 24 figures. 1979-80.

429 - C3PO - 12″ H. Molded metallic plastic figure jointed at hips, shoulders and neck. 1979-80.

430 - R2D2 - 7½″ H. Molded plastic droid has snap-off legs and a "secret compartment" in the back. Pushing panel on front springs open the door to reveal two "programs" in R2's "memory banks." Dome head turns 360° with clicking sound. 1979-80.

431 - BOBA FETT - 13″ H. Molded plastic figure jointed at hips, shoulders, knees, elbows and neck. Flexible vinyl hands turn 360°. Black helmet antenna raises and lowers with clicking sound. Removable brown vinyl cartridge belt, green synthetic fabric cape, removable rocket backpack, laser gun and braided rope. (Gun not shown.) 1979-80.

432 - JAWA - 8¾″ H. Molded plastic figure jointed at hips and shoulders. Flexible vinyl hands turn 360°. Imitation suede cloth fabric cloak, gray plastic gun, brown vinyl ammunition belt. 1979-80.

433 - BEN (OBI-WAN) KENOBI - 12″ H. Vinyl figure jointed at hips, shoulders and neck. Knees bend. White robe has black insert at neck, cloak is imitation brown suede fabric, boots are brown vinyl. Molded plastic light saber is yellow. 1979-80.

434 - STORMTROOPER - 12″ H. Molded plastic figure jointed at hips and shoulders. (Laser rifle not shown.) 1979-80.

435 - HAN SOLO - 12″ H. Vinyl figure jointed at hips, shoulders and neck. Knees bend. Clothing includes: white shirt, black vest and pants, black vinyl gun belt and boots, laser pistol and medal on a ribbon around his neck. 1978-80. Melinda Brickhouse Collection.

436 - DARTH VADER T.I.E. FIGHTER 10½″ x 10″ x 7″. Molded gray plastic T.I.E. fighter has curved solar panels which pop off to simulate battle damage. Tophatch opens and cockpit seat raises and lowers. Red laser cannon light and laser sound are activated by pushing button on rear deck. 1979-80. (Collector's Edition available in 1984.)

437 - MILLENIUM FALCON - 20½″ x 16″. Large molded plastic replica of Han Solo's space ship. Battery operated "battle alert" sounds when button on side is pushed. Opening cockpit canopy, manually operated swivelling radar disc, fold-down entrance ramp, retractable landing skids and lift-off top deck panel. Gun turret and chair spin to produce clicking sound and secret floor panel lifts to reveal smuggling compartment. Simulated game table for "space chess" and a hanging remote "Force" ball are included. 1979-present.

Die Cast Vehicles made in 1979 and 1980 include the Darth Vader T.I.E. Fighter, the Millenium Falcon, and Y-Wing Fighter and Princess Leia's Royal Command Ship. See 1980 Die Cast Vehicles for photo of all vehicles made. 1979-80.

438 - CREATURE CANTINA - 14″ x 8″ base. Molded plastic base piece has two action lever controls for five positions. Swinging doors shown open in this photo. Cardboard background panel. 1979-80.

439 - LAND OF THE JAWAS ACTION PLAYSET - 18½″ x 10″ x 11″ H. Molded plastic base has an action lever to control figures. Cardboard Jawa Sandcrawler background has manually controlled elevator. Plastic "escape pod" included. 1979-80.

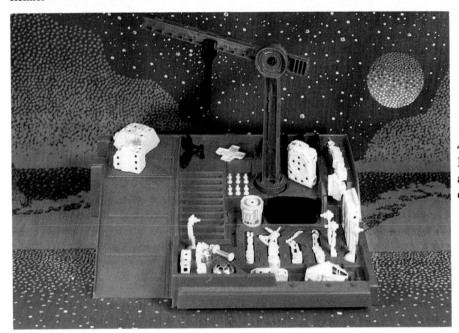

440 - DROID FACTORY - 13″ x 10¾″ base. Molded plastic platform has movable crane and 31 interchangeable pieces to build five different robots at a time. 1979-80.

442 - ELECTRONIC BATTLE COMMAND GAME - 8⅛″ x 6¼″ x 4½″ H. Electronic console with touch control operates on six "AA" batteries or on A.C. adapter, not included. 1979-80.

441 - DESTROY DEATH STAR GAME - Includes: game board with rotating Death Star spinner, four X-Wing squadron bases, and 12 tiny plastic X-Wing fighters, three each in red, green, blue and yellow. 1979-80.

443 - IMPERIAL TROOPER TRANS-PORTER - 10½″ x 5½″. Battery-operated molded plastic replica of Imperial Stormtroopers' "Hovercraft." Six buttons on top activate mechanism which produces corresponding sound for button pushed. Included sounds are: R2D2, the troop transport vehicle, laser fire, stormtrooper and C3PO. 1979-80.

444 - RADIO CONTROLLED JAWA SANDCRAWLER - 16½″ x 5½″ x 8″ H. Molded plastic replica of Jawas' vehicle. Manually operated elevator drops down to transport salvaged droids in or out. 1979-80.

445 - PATROL DEWBACK - 10½″ x 4½″ to top of saddle. Molded plastic lizard has removable saddle and bridle (bridle not shown.) Head and tail move from side to side. 1979-80. (Collectors' Edition available in 1984.)

446 - 1000-PC. JIGSAW PUZZLES - "Star Wars Adventure" and "Aboard the Millenium Falcon." 1979.

447 - 1500-PC. JIGSAW PUZZLE - "Millenium Falcon in Hyper Space," one of two available. 1979.

448 - 500-PC. JIGSAW PUZZLES - SERIES II - "Luke Skywalker and Princess Leia Leap for Their Lives!" and "Darth Vader and Ben Kenobi Duel with Light Sabers!" 1979.

449A and 449B - NEXT 11 ACTION FIGURES: First photo: Luke Skywalker in Bespin Fatigues, Han Solo in Hoth Battle Gear, Rebel Snow Soldier, IG-88, Bossk and Imperial Snow Stormtrooper. Second photo: Black Bespin Security Guard, FX-7, Princess Leia in the Bespin Gown, Lando Calrissian, and White Bespin Security Guard. 1979-present.

450 - "STAR WARS" ACTION FIGURE SURVIVAL KIT - (Mail-in offer.) Twelve accessories include: Luke Skywalker's AT-AT grappling hook (not shown), Jedi blue training harness, two white Hoth backpacks, three translucent Asteroid gas masks, and five assorted laser weapons. 1980. (Offer expired May 31, 1981.)

451 - DARTH VADER COLLECTOR'S CASE - 16″ x 15¼″ H. Hinged, molded plastic case holds 31 action figures and accessories. 1980-present.

452 - TWIN POD CLOUD CAR - 10″ x 9″ x 3½″ (skids retracted). Molded plastic space vehicle has opening hatches and retractable landing skids. 1980-81.

453 - REBEL ARMORED SNOWSPEEDER - 12½″ L. (including harpoon gun) x 10½″ W.. Molded plastic vehicle with opening hatch cover and button-controlled landing skid. Battery-controlled pulsating lights and laser sound. Removable harpoon. 1980-82.

454 - DIECAST TWIN POD CLOUD CAR - 3¾″ x 3¼″. Miniature cast metal model of the ship. Retractable landing skids. c. 1980-81. Other diecast models available were: Darth Vader's Star Destroyer (1980), T.I.E. Bomber, (1980), Slave I, (1980-81), and Snowspeeder, (1980-81). These diecast vehicles as well as all others are shown in the following photo.

455 - IG-88 - 15″ H. Silvery gray plastic robot bounty hunter is jointed at neck, shoulders, wrists and hips. Accessories include: black plastic laser rifle and laser pistol, and brown vinyl cartridge belt holding four orange plastic cartridges. 1980.

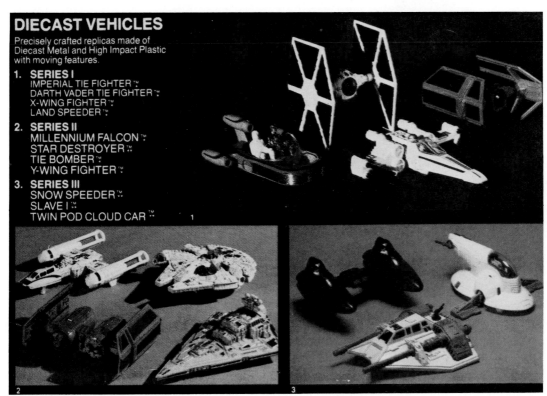

DIECAST VEHICLES
Precisely crafted replicas made of Diecast Metal and High Impact Plastic with moving features.

1. **SERIES I**
IMPERIAL TIE FIGHTER
DARTH VADER TIE FIGHTER
X-WING FIGHTER
LAND SPEEDER

2. **SERIES II**
MILLENNIUM FALCON
STAR DESTROYER
TIE BOMBER
Y-WING FIGHTER

3. **SERIES III**
SNOW SPEEDER
SLAVE I
TWIN POD CLOUD CAR

456 - Page from 1980 "Empire" booklet showing all die cast vehicles ever available.

457 - HOTH ICE PLANET ADVENTURE SET - Background: 12″ x 17″. Playset includes: three-dimensional printed cardboard background AT-AT with manually operated elevator, 4″ H. gray plastic radar laser cannon and molded light gray plastic foreground terrain, which supports background. 1980.

458 - IMPERIAL ATTACK BASE PLAYSET - Base: 17″ x 9½″ x 3″ H.. Eight-piece molded plastic playset simulates the ice planet Hoth environment. Features include an exploding command post, collapsing ice bridge and movable gun. 1980-81.

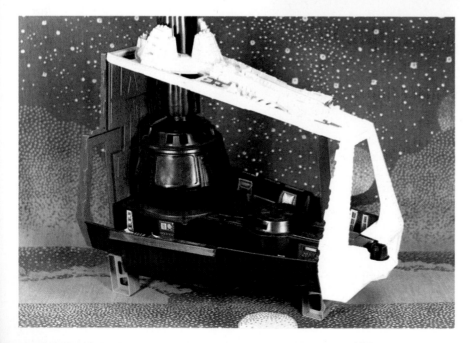

459 - DARTH VADER'S STAR DESTROYER - 15″ L. (without gun) x 10″ W. A play environment of molded plastic includes a meditation chamber with battery-operated light, a simulated hologram (red rectangle), secret escape hatch and movable gun (missing from photo.) 1980.

460 - TAUNTAUN - Approximately 6" H. Molded plastic Hoth Snow Creature with removable vinyl saddle and bridle. (Tauntaun lying down is the 1982 open-belly version. Note the wider cinch strap on the saddle.) 1980-81.

KEYSTONE MFG. CO.

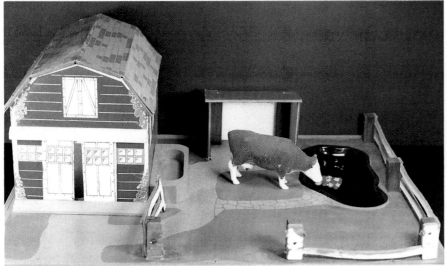

461 - KEYSTONE MFG. CO. FARM SET - 16" x 22" base. Made of masonite and Tekwood, the base, barn, trough, shed and fence are fastened together. The rubber cow "drinks" water when squeezed, then gives milk. Pond is translucent blue plastic. Also included in the set, but not shown, were: magnetic fishing pole and two fish, two floating ducks, milk pail, rubber sow and two piglets who suckled due to inner magnets. c. 1952. Price in 1952 - $4.98.

KIDDIE BRUSH & TOY CO.

462 - SUZY GOOSE CARPET SWEEPER - Base: 8" L. x 5½" W.; handle 18" L. Metal litho top is nailed to wooden end pieces where red wooden wheels are fastened on. Stiff fiber brush picks up dirt. Wooden handle is held by heavy metal wire bracket. (Part of a cleaning set.) c. 1948-50.

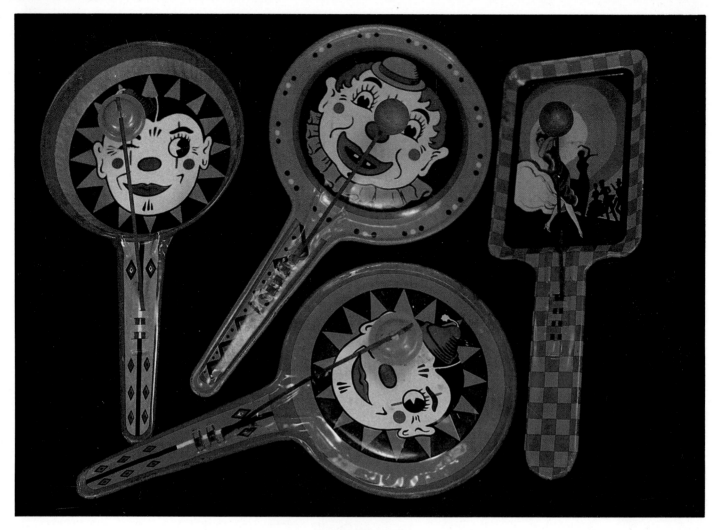

KIRCHHOF

463 - ASSORTMENT OF NOISEMAKERS - 8″ x 8¾″ L. All are metal litho; two have red wooden ball clappers, two have yellow metal clappers. Original price - 10¢.

464 - HALLOWEEN NOISEMAKERS - Witch head: 4″ across. Cylinder: 3″ high. Both are metal litho with pink wooden handles.

"JOY OF A TOY - KNICKERBOCKER"

This company is probably best known for its stuffed Raggedy Ann and Andy dolls and Sesame Street characters.

465 - MELODIE BELLS - Each 3½″ H. Brittle plastic bell-shaped housings hold tuned metal bells inside. According to Connie Ronningen, these were c. 1950 and were endorsed by Miss Frances of the TV show "Ding Dong School."

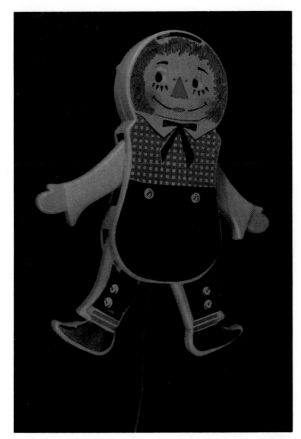

467 - ROOSTER RATTLES - 4½″ H. Pair of pink brittle plastic rattles. Also made in white.

466 - RAGGEDY ANDY "JUMP 'N' SQUEAK" - 9″ H. x 6¼″ W. Paper lithos over plastic body, painted hands. Pulling cord makes arms and legs go up and down, eyes go back and forth, squeaking sound.

468 - SESAME STREET FIRE ENGINE - 6″ L. x 2½″ H. Red plastic fire engine is driven by small stuffed fabric Bert.

469 - AIRPORT PLAYSET - All plastic base with control tower that turns and clicks. Removable propeller fits both plane and helicopter.

KREST

470 - KREST CHILDREN'S KITCHEN SET - Eight-piece child's cooking utensil set is steel. Courtesy of Mr. and Mrs. Vic Newman.

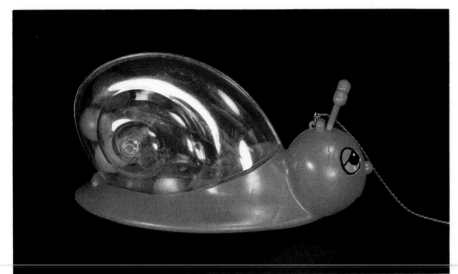

KUSAN

471 - ZOODLE SNAIL - 12″ x 6¼″ x 6″ H. Plastic snail with clear shell holds seven primary colored plastic balls which roll around shell as snail is pulled. Paper litho eyes. c. 1975.

472 - COOTIE POCKET WATCH - 4½″ Dia. Plastic watch has clear face and back. Multi-colored gears can be seen working. Familiar "Cootie" is pictured on the front.

473 - KOO ZOO BLOCK SET - Twelve 1½″ cubes have five clear sides and one solid. Each contains a fixed plastic animal and a small metal bell for a rattle. c. 1957.

474 - LIL' DRILL - 8″ L. Brightly colored plastic drill has three interchangeable bits.

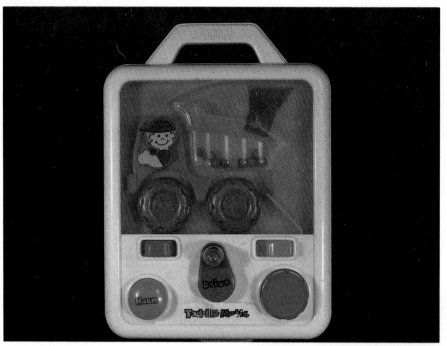

LANARD

475 - LANARD "TODDLE MATIC DUMP TRUCK" - All plastic manipulation toy. Drive crank makes wheels go, red knob loads truck, yellow slide dumps load, red slide rocks driver. c. 1980.

LAPIN

476 - LAPIN TRUCK - 4½" x 1¾" x 1⅝" H. Yellow brittle plastic truck has gray plastic wheels and axles. c. 1955.

LINDSTROM

477 - LINDSTROM SEWING MACHINE - 6" H. x 8" L. x 5" W. Metal litho sewing machine has wooden handle on wheel. c. 1940.

LORRAINE

478 - LORRAINE NOVELTY MFG. CO. INC. "JACK-IN-THE-BOX" - 5¾" x 5¾" x 5¾". Metal litho box has octagonal lid and plastic knob on crank. Jester's head is brittle plastic with air brushed features; body is cloth. Song: "Pop! Goes the Weasel."

SAMUEL LOWE

479 - SAMUEL LOWE'S "MAGNET METAL PICK-UPS" - Box is 7⅞" H., 1⅝" Dia. Set consists of 21 metal "sticks" and a small magnet. Similar to "pick-up-sticks" games, sticks are picked up one at a time--with the magnet in this version--without moving another stick. c. 1941.

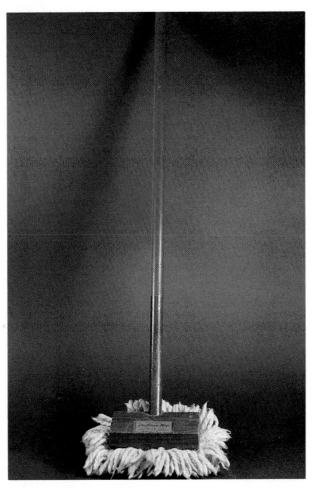

MAGIC MOP

480 - THE MAGIC MOP DUST MOP - 4" x 2" mop head holder, 21" handle. All wooden mop with white cotton mop head. Pat. date Sept. 11, 1945.

MARX TOYS

Louis Marx, born in 1896, was the son of German immigrant parents. An early job with the firm of Ferdinand Strauss, a major early 1900s toymaker, got him started in the "toy game." After Marx made his way up to become a director in the company, a fateful disagreement over a policy decision led to his being fired. Marx' next job was as a salesman for a manufacturer of wooden toys in Vermont. While he was busily increasing the sales of his new firm, he went into partnership with his brother, David, and the two became wholesalers for several manufacturers. After World War I, Marx and his brother bought dies and molds from the old Strauss company, which had gone bankrupt. The molds were modified, different painting designs were used, and the same toys Strauss had made bore the new Marx name. By the time he was 25, Louis Marx was a millionaire. The Marx Company flourished and produced a bewildering assortment of toys for many years. One of Marx' most famous inventions has to be the yo-yo, but the windups and playsets are most favored by collectors. Living by a strict business code, Louis Marx succeeded in a grand manner by providing good quality toys at a low price. In the late 1950s, he sold Marx Toys to the Quaker Oats Company for $31.3 million and retired. Marx initiated only one trend during the 1970s--the "Big Wheel" tricycles. Toy soldiers and war playsets had been a big part of Louis Marx' business; but, due to the prevailing anti-war sentiment of the 60s and 70s, Quaker dropped those toys from the line. In 1978, Quaker sold Marx to Dunbee-Combex, a British toy firm. For whatever reasons, the new owners did no better; and Marx Toys filed for bankruptcy in 1980. Louis Marx died in February of 1982.

481 - HOPPING RABBIT - 4½" Windup metal litho rabbit carries a carrot as he hops along. Separate ears and "cotton" tail.

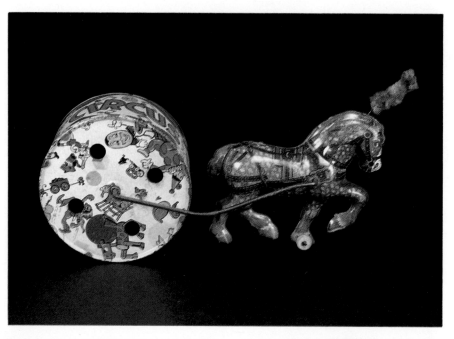

482 - MUSICAL CIRCUS HORSE - 10" L. x 4¼" H. Metal litho horse rolls on two wooden wheels. Mechanism inside drum makes a tinkling sound as it rolls along between metal shafts. Plume on horse's head is plush fibers wound in wire.

484 - THE MICKEY MOUSE EXPRESS - Metal litho windup train runs around track, through tunnels and over bridge. c. 1940. Courtesy of Jim Yeager.

483 - PINOCCHIO WALKER -Metal litho windup whose eyes move up and down. A less desirable version had non-moving eyes. c. 1940. Courtesy of Jim Yeager.

485 - GEORGE THE DRUMMER BOY - Metal litho windup toy with original box. Walks and beats drum. Courtesy of Jim Yeager.

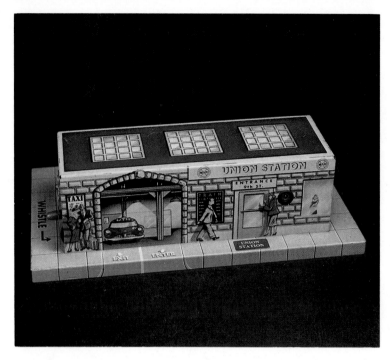

486 - TRAIN STATION WITH WHISTLE - Platform: 9″ x 5¼″.
Station: 2¾″ H. Metal litho platform and station. Whistle
operates on two "D" batteries. c. 1940s.

487 - THE BIG PARADE - 15″ L. x 11½″ H. (to top
of hat.) Battery-operated brittle plastic toy. Soldiers
have removable hats and guns (missing in photo) and
march to cadence swinging left arms up and down.
Moving pennant on top of drum left or right makes
toy move in the opposite direction. c. 1960s.

488A and 488B - ELECTRO ART - Similar to the more familiar "Lite Brite" by Hasbro. This version has a storage drawer
for six colors of pegs as well as a see-through plastic tracer tray to convert the unit into a light table. 1960s.

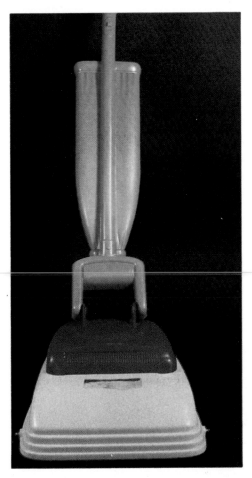

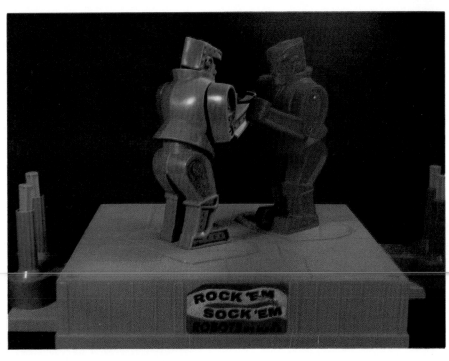

491 - ROCK-EM SOCK-EM ROBOTS - 14″ sq. yellow plastic base; robots: 9″ tall. Push button controls on sides maneuver robots and throw punches-- heads pop up when direct hit is scored. (White plastic ring ropes missing in photo.) c. 1974.

489 - VACUUM SWEEPER - Base: 9″ x 11½″ x 4″; handle: 22″ L.. Molded plastic base has red plastic wheels and metal diaphragm noisemaker hidden underneath. Molded blue plastic bag and handle.

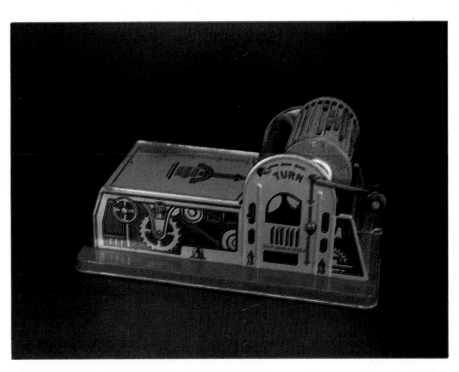

492 - HAND OPERATED PRINTING PRESS -10¼″ x 6″x 5″ H. Metal litho printing press uses rubber type. Bell rings as each piece of paper is printed and rolled out.

490 - GOOFY - 7″ H. Hollow plastic head, body, hands and feet connected by vinyl-covered wire. Fabric clothing.

493 - JUNIOR TYPEWRITER - 11³/₈″ across carriage; 7⁵/₈″ W., 4½″ H. Metal litho base, metal carriage and dial face, plastic knobs and type dial. c. 1957. Price in 1957 - $3.77.

494 - PET SHOP DELIVERY TRUCK - 10¾″ x 3½″ x 4″ H. Brittle plastic truck has lift sides with compartments on each side for hard rubber dogs. c. 1950.

495 - "RIVER QUEEN" PADDLE-WHEELER - 8½″ L. x 4″ W. x 3½″ H. Brittle plastic paddle wheel steamboat. (Not a water toy.)

496 - BOP-A-BEAR - 13″ x 7″ x 9½″ H. (This is part of a set which included a suction cup dart-shooting double-barrelled rifle and six darts.) Hollow plastic bear has large battery operated mechanism inside. Bear rolls forward until hit with dart, then growls and turns. c. 1963. Price in 1963 - $7.99.

497 - "MARXWRITER" TYPEWRITER - 11″ x 11″ x 4½″. Working "real" typewriter is mostly plastic with some metal parts. Most recent model in a long line of Marx typewriters.

499 - FORT APACHE - Playset includes: metal litho H.Q. building with plastic porch, 41 cavalry figures, 15 Indians, campfire, chopping block, cord wood, cookstand, catwalks, blockhouses, stockade fence, well, tepee, totem pole, horses. c. 1974. Price in 1974 - $8.49. (Fort Apache playsets were available in several sizes.)

498 - GUNS OF NAVARONE - Over 200-piece playset includes a 17″ x 10½″ x 25″ molded gray plastic mountain and a 32″ x 36″ vinyl playmat. c. 1976. (The same mold was used for the jungle mountain in the 1979 "Iwo Jima" playset.)

500 - LAZY DAY FARMS BARN - 13¾″ x 9¼″ x 11″. Many of Marx' farm sets used this same barn with different lithography on each one. Cupolas are plastic. (Note the nice interior detail.)

501 - "MICKEY AND FRIENDS" HOUSE - 12″ L. x 9″ W. x 9″ H. Metal litho house with white plastic handle and dormer windows may have originally been part of a playset. Courtesy of Dr. L. F. Culley.

502A and 502B - FIRE STATION #303 - Base: 17" x 11", 11½" H. Metal litho fire station has two garage doors that raise and lower. Crank on side makes fire engine roll out when turned. Beautifully detailed interior includes map of city, roster sheet, calendar, lockers, fire extinguishers, various awards and certificates, fireplace and firemen's equipment. (This piece came from the engineering department of Marx Toys. Masking tape marks above the door show where its identifying information label once was. This, too, may have been a playset.)

503A - SKY-VIEW PARKING PLAYSET - Base: 26¼″ x 14¾″. This M.I.B. set has never been assembled. The main play piece is metal litho and is made from ten separate tabbed pieces that fit together. Accessory pieces with lugs snap into holes in base. The following photos show the components in detail. c. 1954. Price in 1954 - $2.99.

503B - Grease Rack and Wash Rack.

503C - Accessories; clockwise from left: sink, commode, tool bench, two gas pumps, bucket and sponge, water can, oil rack, air pump and grease pump.

503D - Cars and Wheels.

503E - Original Box.

504A - FARM SET - Includes (1) metal litho barn, one-piece side and ends, one-piece roof, floor piece, loft piece; (2) metal litho silo with plastic top; (3) many accessories. Following photos show pieces in detail. c. 1963.

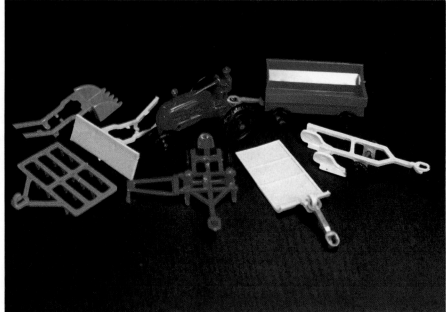

504B - Tractor and Implements - Clockwise from center: tractor and wagon, gang plow, stone boat, corn planter, spiked tooth harrow, scraper blade and scoop.

504C - Two hay bales, two feed sacks, milking stool and pail, covered trash can, scoop shovel, pitchfork and feed box with hinged lid.

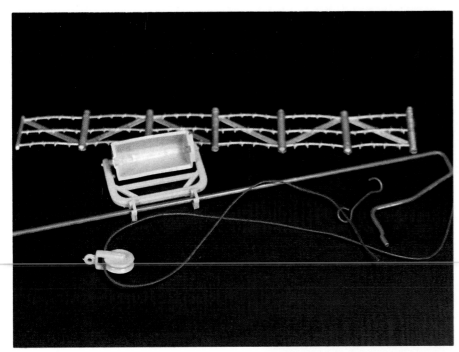

504D - Two sections of snap-together barbed wire fence (ten included), litter carrier and track assembly, hook and pulley assembly.

504E - Horse and foal, goat and kid, two cows and a calf, three lambs, dog, sow and two pigs. (Animals standing on original box.)

504F - Six farm workers.

505 - MEDIEVAL CASTLE - Large playset with knights and vikings. Combination metal litho and plastic; vacuuform plastic base. Courtesy of Chuck Saults.

506 - LAZY DAY FARMS TRUCK - 18″ L. x 6½″ W. x 5¾″ H. Metal litho truck has black plastic tires marked "Lumar."

507 - TRUCK CAB - 5″ x 4¾″ x 4½″ H. Dark blue metal litho truck cab with corrections noted on it is from the Marx engineering department.

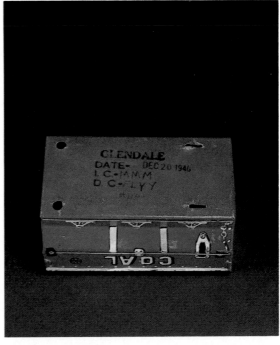

508A and 508B - COAL TRUCK BED - This sample from the Louis Marx engineering department is an original, hand painted prototype. The Marx logo is a small decal which has been applied. c. 1940.

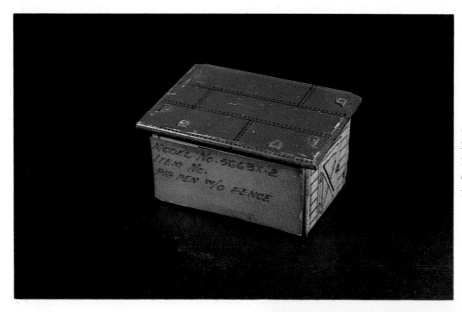

509 - PIG PEN WITHOUT FENCE - 3½″ x 2¼″ x 1⁷/₈″″ H. This metal litho sample farm building is from the engineering department of Louis Marx, as are the following six photos.

510A and 510B - PIG PEN WITH FENCE -5″ x 3½″ x 1⁷/₈″ H.

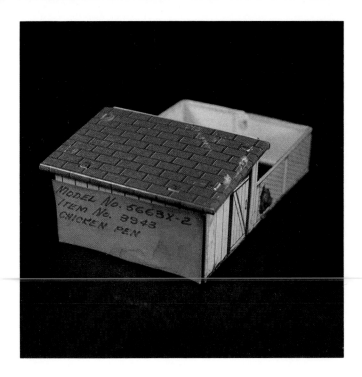

511 (left) and 511 (below) - CHICKEN PEN - 5″ x 3½″ x 1⁷/₈″ H.

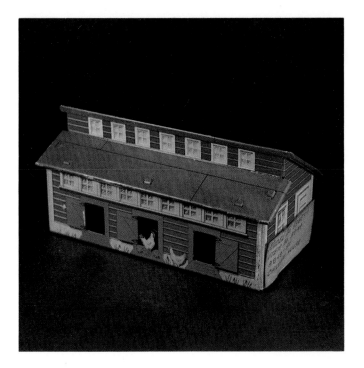

512 (above) and 512 (right) - CHICKEN HOUSE - 7½″ x 3¾″ x 3½″ H.

513 - HORSE AND BUCKBOARD - Overall length: 24″; horse, 13″ tall. Molded plastic horse with soft vinyl harness pulls plastic buckboard. This was an accessory piece for the "Johnny West" group of action figures. c. 1973.

514 - JOHNNY WEST HORSES - Pancho, Thunderbolt and Buckskin. Other horses in the series were: Comanche and Storm-cloud. The Johnny West Adventure Series figures (besides Chief Cherokee) were: Johnny West, Jay West, Jane West, Janice West, Josie West, Sheriff Garrett, Sam Cobra, Jed Gibson, General Custer, Captain Maddox, Geronimo, Fighting Eagle and Wildflower. Besides the horse and buckboard pictured, a horse and covered wagon was also available.

515 - CHIEF CHEROKEE -Figure: 11½″ tall. Jointed molded plastic figure comes with 30 pieces of gear including: eagle feather headdress, spirit rattle, tomahawk, war club, ceremonial mask, bear claw necklace, beaded belt, knife and sheath, bone breastplate, leather shield, peace pipe, hackamore, saddle blanket and cinch, eagle feather headband, rifle, spear, tom-tom and drumstick, quiver and six arrows, bow, wampum belt, buffalo horn headdress, parfleche and strap. c. 1975.

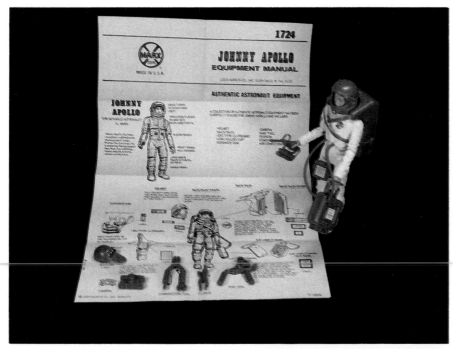

516 - JOHNNY APOLLO - 7½" H. Fully articulated molded vinyl astronaut figure comes with ten separate accessories including: helmet, backpack, air conditioning unit, guidance gun, leg-type clipboard, long-billed cap, camera, combination tool "plench", and nab tool. c. 1968.

517 - SLANT BOARD WALKERS - Zebra: 3½" x 3" H. These little plastic toys walk either on an inclined surface or across a horizontal one when a weighted string is attached to the eye of those so equipped. (Only the Zebra and Stegasaurus have eyes in this group.) c. 1950s.

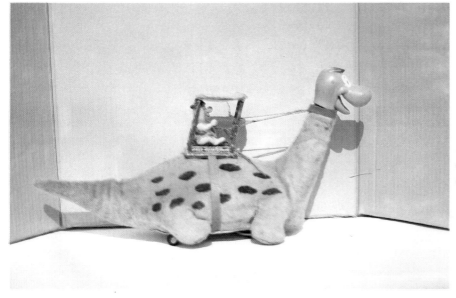

518 - DINO THE DINOSAUR AND FRED FLINTSTONE - 22" L. This battery-operated toy has eight actions. c. 1961. Courtesy of Jean Couch. Photo by Jerry Couch.

YOU CAN TELL IT'S MATTEL - IT'S SWELL!

After a successful first business venture of designing light fixtures, jewelry, and plastic novelties, Elliot Handler branched off into a new area--manufacturing doll furniture. This step, taken in 1945, was the first in a series of events which would lead to the creation of Mattel, Inc. Mr. Handler and his partners disagreed about the future of their company; and, as a result, Mr. Handler sold his interest. With an old friend, Harold Matson, Elliot Handler started Mattel Creations--"Matt" for Matson and "El" for Elliot. A few additional plastic toys were added to the doll furniture line in 1946, and Mattel was incorporated in 1948 in California. One of the two ideas which made Mattel's fortunes happened in 1955: Mattel decided to buy network time to advertise toys to children. The result was that, for the first time, both the toy and the manufacturer were sold directly to the consumer. The second idea came only four years later. The product was initiated by Ruth Handler, Elliot's wife, and named after his daughter--Barbie. The new doll's reception at the 1959 New York Toy Show was an overwhelming "It'll never sell." The Barbie Doll is now, of course, the most famous doll in history.

519 - MERRY-GO-ROUND - 7″ H. x 7″ Dia. base. Metal litho base and umbrella top, brittle plastic animals and striped cardboard center post. Animals revolve to "Oh, Dear, What Can The Matter Be?" when handle is turned. (Three animals missing from this toy.) c. 1952.

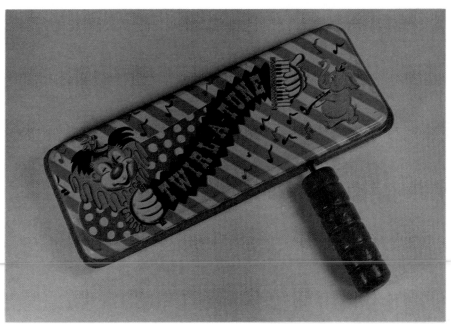

520 - TWIRL-A-TUNE - 8¼″ x 3¼″ x 3″ handle. Metal litho "music maker toy" with turned wooden handle. c. 1951.

521 - COWBOY GE-TAR AND MUSIC BOX - 14″ L. Black plastic guitar has western decals on front, attached shoulder strap and wire strings. Turning handle on side plays "Red River Valley." c. 1952.

522 - MUSIC BOX EGG - 6″ H. Metal litho egg holds music box mechanism that plays "Here Comes Peter Cottontail." c. 1953.

523 - PETER COTTONTAIL MUSICAL EASTER BASKET - Basket: 5¼″ x 4″ x 2½″ H. Handle: 2″ H. Cardboard basket has printed paper covering and yellow plastic handle. Metal plate inside basket covers music box mechanism. Basket could be bought either empty or filled with paper-covered candy eggs. (Ducks and chickens shown here are of the period but were made in Japan.) c. 1955.

524 - SCARECROW-IN-THE-MUSIC-BOX - 5¼″ x 5¼″ x5½″. Metal litho box. Scarecrow has brittle plastic head and hat, fabric body and flexible vinyl hands. Tune is "Hail, Hail, the Gang's All Here." c. 1967.

525 - SNOOPY-IN-THE-MUSIC-BOX - 5¼″ x 5¼″ x 5½″. Metal litho box, plastic handle on crank. Snoopy's body is cloth, paws are flexible vinyl hands, brittle plastic head with moving eyes. Tune is "Where, Oh! Where, Has My Little Dog Gone?" c. 1966.

526 - JACK-IN-THE-MUSIC-BOX - 5¼″ x 5¼″ x 5½″. Metal litho box, wooden knob on the crank, fabric clothing, flexible vinyl hands, brittle plastic head with moving eyes. Tune is "Mulberry Bush." c. 1961. Price in 1961 - $2.50.

528 - JACK-IN-THE-MUSIC-BOX - 5¼″ x 5¼″ x 5½″. Metal litho music box plays "Mulberry Bush." Clown has plastic head, flexible vinyl hands and cloth body. c. 1971.

527 - GIRAFFE-IN-THE-MUSIC-BOX - 5¼″ x 5¼″ x 5½″. Metal litho box plays "The Bear Went Over the Mountain." Giraffe has plastic head with felt ears and a cloth body. c. 1967.

529 - TALKING CLOWN-IN-THE-MUSIC-BOX - 5¼″ x 5¼″ x 5½″. Metal litho box. Pushing orange button on front makes clown jump up. Pulling white ring plays recorded statements like: "Whew! it was hot in there!," "Let's go to the circus!," "Let's clown around," etc. c. 1971.

530 - MOTHER GOOSE-IN-THE-MUSIC-BOX - 5¼″ x 5¼″ x 5½″. Metal litho box. "Mother Goose" has brittle plastic head and hat, flexible vinyl hands and cloth body. c. 1971.

531 - BUGS BUNNY TALKING HAND PUPPET - Gray and white plush fabric hand puppet has vinyl face. Pull string talker is in front. c. 1968.

532 - TOG'L TOY CHEST - One set of Mattel's building block system of small colored plastic cubes, one side of which is hinged and opens. Various arrangements of holes and pegs on all sides. Also included are axles, pinion gears, wheels, panels and an air pump. c. 1969.

533 - SPACE MISSION TEAM - Figures: 6″ H. Molded rubber-like vinyl figures are bendable and poseable. This set includes: Major Matt Mason (white), Sgt. Storm, (red), Doug Davis (gold) and Callisto (green), plus these accessories: white space sled, red trac, and Callisto's "space sensor" device. c. 1970.

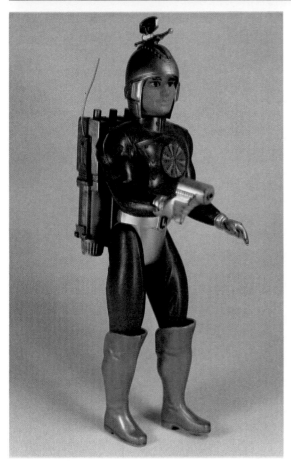

535 - SPACE CRAWLER - 14″ x 8″ x 8″ H. Battery-operated plastic vehicle moves forward and has winch mechanism. Major Matt Mason figure fits in seat. 1966-1970.

534 - CAPTAIN LAZER - 13″ H. with helmet. "Major Matt Mason's Friend From Outer Space" is jointed at neck, shoulders, hips and knees. His battery-powered pack has three push buttons to operate his flashing eyes, solar chest panel and laser pistol. (Came with three accessories for pistol: Cosmic Beam, Paralyzer Wand and Radiation Shield.) Also came with removable helmet (shown) and lunar surface space treader boots (not shown). c. 1968-70.

536A - BUILD-A-TRAIN - 8″ L. x 5½″ H. Four wooden parts, four wooden wheels and eight plastic pegs go together to make a train engine. (Came with wooden claw hammer.) A tractor and ship were also available. c. 1971.

536B - BUILD-A-TRAIN - disassembled.

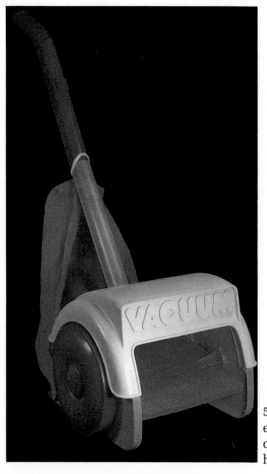

537 - TUFF-STUFF VACUUM - Base: 9″ x 8″ x 7″ H. Handle: 19″ L. Molded plastic upright vacuum cleaner picks up debris with a rotating sheet of closed cell foam. Orange cloth bag removes for emptying. Two-section handle. c. 1974-present.

538 - TUFF-STUFF NUMBERS - Multi-colored blocky numbers made of Mattel's heavy "tuff-stuff" material. A set consists of two of each numeral. Tuff-Stuff letters are also available. Set consists of one of each letter plus an extra A, E, I and O.

539 - CRACKFIRE FIRECRACKER - 5½" H. x 2¼" Dia. Plastic firecracker has printed paper strip glued on. Fuse is braided string, and cast metal firing mechanism is in the base. Circular plastic "strip" caps are used for ammunition, one at a time. "Bang" is accompanied by a whistling sound. c. 1975.

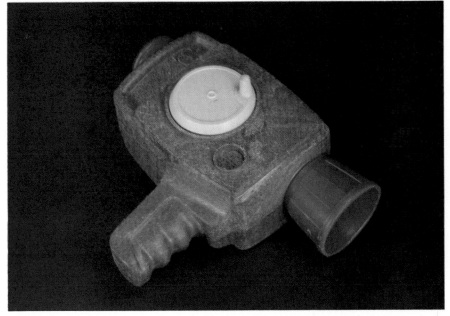

540 - TUFF-STUFF MOVIE CAMERA - Turning crank makes a kaleidoscopic effect. c. 1975.

541 - PUTT-PUTT ''ALL ABOARD'' MOTOR RAILROAD - Set includes: 8-pc. track, two loading platforms, train station, covered bridge, swinging crossing guard, 3-pc. wind-up train and two Putt-Putt people. c. 1976. (A variety of Putt-Putt sets were available through the 1970s.)

542 - PULSAR - 13½″ H. Plastic jointed figure has clear plastic chest through which heart, lungs, and circulatory system are visible. Pressing back plate makes ''blood'' flow, lungs ''breathe'' and heart ''beat.'' Two-piece head is hinged at the top. When face is lifted, computer brain is exposed. One of two ''mission'' discs can be put in place to ''program'' Pulsar. Also available was a ''Life System Center,'' a pretend energizing and programming machine which contains an X-ray screen, power pak and scanner, circuitry connections and a control panel.

543 - TOOL BOX - 12″ x 8″ x 7″. Tool box and many accessories are all plastic. c. 1978.

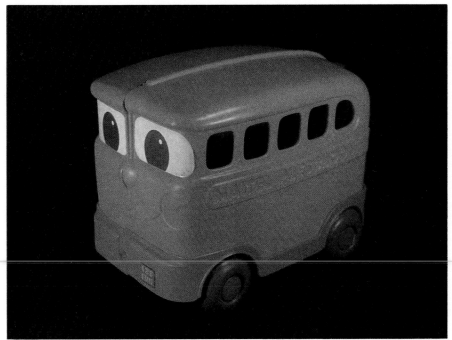

544A and 544B - PRESCHOOL BUS PLAYSET - Includes: yellow and orange plastic bus storage case; orange teeter-totter; blue wavy slide; two weighted figures on dual wheels; car, plane and deck pieces which snap onto figures, and yellow rolling hoop (not shown.) c. 1978.

545 - BUGS BUNNY-IN-THE-MUSIC-BOX - 5¼″ x 5¼″ x 5½″. Plastic box has paper litho on four sides. Plastic handle on crank. Bug's head is brittle plastic, his hands and ears are flexible vinyl and his body is cloth. c. 1978-80.

546 - SOF-TUFF DUMP TRUCK - 7″ x 5″ x 4½″ H. One of a line of soft molded foam-like toys. Rolls on hard plastic wheels and axles. c. 1978.

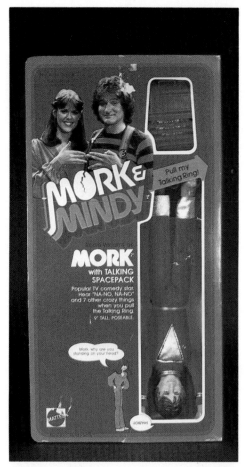

547 - "MORK" WITH TALKING SPACEPACK - 9″ Jointed vinyl figure in red stretch space suit. Has pull-string talker in "spacepack" that fits on his back. Gray space boots. c. 1979.

548 - CALLIOPE - Yellow and blue "pumper" rod inflates balloon inside net bag; keys then play on bagpipe principle. All plastic. Comes with color coded song book. c. 1980. Courtesy of Tom Johnson.

MEGO

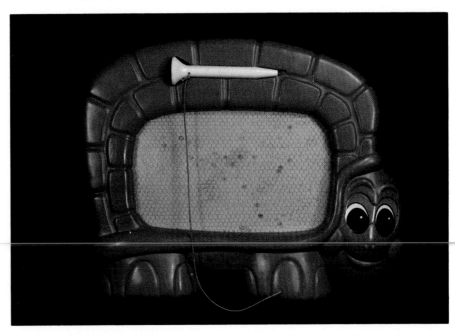

549 - THE HULK - 7″ H. One of many Mego "Superhero" action figures. All came with appropriate clothing. c. 1970s.

550 - TOODLE DOODLE TURTLE - Magnetic pen "writes" on special slate in center of plastic turtle frame. "Eraser" magnet rubbed across back removes writing. c. 1980.

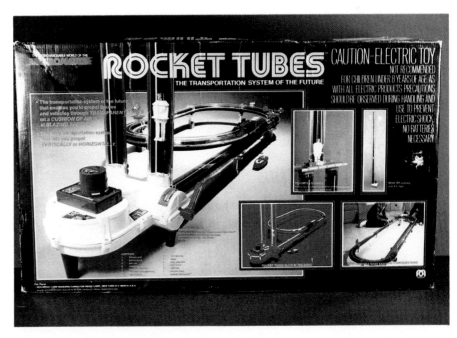

551 - MICRONAUTS "TIME TRAVEL-LER" - 3¾″ H. One of the set of poseable action figures in the very large Micronaut line of toys. c. 1976.

552 - MICRONAUT ROCKET TUBES - The transportation system for the Micronaut line (operated by electricity.) 57-pc. set. c. 1979.

553 - MICRORAIL CITY - Monorail system for "Micropolis." 232-pc. set. c. 1978.

METAL MASTERS

554 - METAL MASTERS "POPEYE & SWEET PEA XYLOPHONE" - Paper lithos on wood and painted wood pull toy is hinged in the center and has metal wheels. c. 1940s. Metal Masters also made riding toys.

NEWTON MANUFACTURING COMPANY

This company doing business in Newton, Iowa, since 1909, specializes in advertising items. The "Aero Circus," manufactured for only a couple of years during the early 1930s was their main entry in the toy field. According to senior marketing V.P. John McNeer, the company also manufactured jigsaw puzzles, felt pennants and kids' "beanie" caps at one time. A toy familiar to everyone, the "Ding-Bat" or "Paddle Ball"--a rubber ball attached to a wooden paddle by a piece of elastic--originated at the Newton Manufacturing Company.

555 - NEWTON AERO CIRCUS - Original box. c. 1931.

556 - NEWTON AERO CIRCUS - When toy is assembled, the weight of the cast iron blimp falling down the center pole causes the two wood, paper and cast iron planes to circle upward. When the blimp reaches bottom, it automatically disconnects. The planes then reverse direction and land.

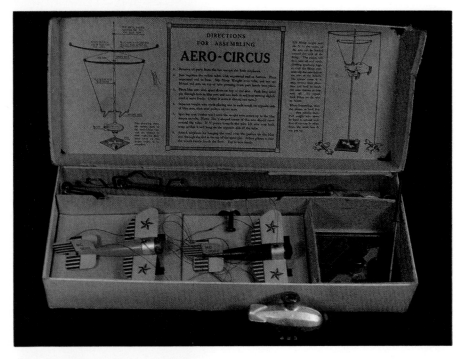

NOMA

557 - NOMA TUMBLE CLOWNS - 3¾" H. Brittle plastic clowns are recessed on both sides to hold paper litho pictures. c. 1950.

Noma Toys catalog pictures from late 1940s. Courtesy of Candy Bohn.

You will love this black and white cocker-spaniel. So real, so life-like. Actually walks along behind you when pulled . . 11" long. He's the NOMA Walking Dog every child wants—No. 756.

This waddling, walking duck is adorable too—with orange legs and bill. Follows you around when pulled. It's the NOMA Walking Duck—No. 756 DK.

What fun! Big 21½" NOMA dump truck. Body raises, gate slides out—No. 751 S. Oh boy! The NOMA tractor makes noise like a real motor . . . 8½" long. Has large driving wheels—No. 755 T.

558X - WALKING DOG   **559X - WALKING DUCK**   **560X - DUMP TRUCK AND TRACTOR**

NOMA Woodie Train—30" long. Brightly colored locomotive, tender, gondola and caboose—No. 753.
Get your garage ready for the gay NOMA Woodie oil and ice trucks. 6 wheels, 11¾" long—No. 752 and 752 LT.

Be a railroad man. Here's a six car deluxe NOMA train, locomotive, tender, box car, tank car, coal car and caboose . . 54" long—No. 754.
NOMA Flyer . . . 25½" long. Moving drive rods, flanged wheels—No. 754 P.

Girls, here's fun. NOMA Hickory-Dickory Dock. Mice move up and down, clock turns, bell rings, marbles fall. 14" high—No. 777. For little shavers—NOMA Rolly Ducky . . . 9" long. Bobs up and down—No. 760.

561X - WOODIE TRAIN, OIL TRUCK, ICE TRUCK   **562X - 754 TRAIN, NOMA FLYER**   **563X - HICKORY DICKORY DOCK & ROLLY DUCKY**

N. N. HILL BRASS CO.

The company in this instance bears the founder's name - N. N. Hill. Begun in 1889, this was one of four bell companies located in East Hampton, Connecticut, at that time. The toys made by N. N. Hill Brass were similar in design to those made by their friendly competitor, Gong Bell. Wyman Hill was president of the company when it was sold in 1960, and toys were made by them until that time. (Information courtesy of Carl Feist, former Vice President and General Manager of the company; and his wife, Catherine, granddaughter of the founder.)

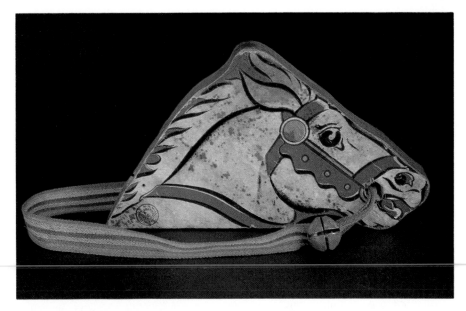

564 - STICK HORSE - Head only: 7½" x 4". Paper lithos on wood horse head was originally nailed onto ½" Dia. dowel inserted into hole in back of neck. Multi-colored twill reins have a bell on each side. A slightly larger head was also made which was attached to a square stick with bell wheels on either side.

565 - HORSE BELL TOY - 13" L. x 5½" H. Paper lithos on wooden horse with wooden front wheels. Wooden shafts connect to large metal bell wheels. Courtesy of Betty Jane Updike.

566 - DOG BELL TOY - Similar to horse above. Courtesy of Betty Barry.

THE OHIO ART COMPANY

The Ohio Art Company began in October of 1908 when Henry S. Winzeler hired eight people to make metal picture frames in the rented second floor of the Archbold, Ohio Band Hall. The enterprise proved successful; and by 1910, the company was producing 20,000 picture frames each day. Because of the need to expand facilities, the company moved to Bryan and the new plant began production February 2, 1912. A few small wagons and windmills were the first toys produced. World War I stopped the importing of German toys, and Ohio Art greatly expanded its line to fill the gap. The well-known tea sets were introduced in 1920. In 1969, Ohio Art purchased Emenee Industries, manufacturers of toy musical instruments. Since the 1920s, Ohio Art has consistently manufactured these toys: tops, drums, sand pails and shovels, tea sets, watering cans, snow shovels and globes.

567 - MINIATURE BABY BUGGY - 7″ L. The wheels on this metal litho buggy are not original--the originals were smaller and nickle plated. c. 1930. Courtesy of Jean Couch. Photo by Jerry Couch.

568 - DRUM - 11″ Dia., 5″ H. Metal litho drum has fabric heads, twill neck-strap and wooden drum sticks. c. 1942.

206

569 - ROY ROGERS HORSESHOE SET - Set consists of two metal litho bases 7″ Dia. (shown here) with 2¾″ L. nickel plated metal studs and one pair each of red and black flexible vinyl horseshoes, 5¼″ L. c. mid-1950s.

570 - ROY ROGERS RANCH LANTERN - 7½″ H., 5″ wire handle; base 4″ Dia. Metal litho lantern with clear plastic chimney; 1½ volt flashlight bulb operates on one "D" battery. c. 1956.

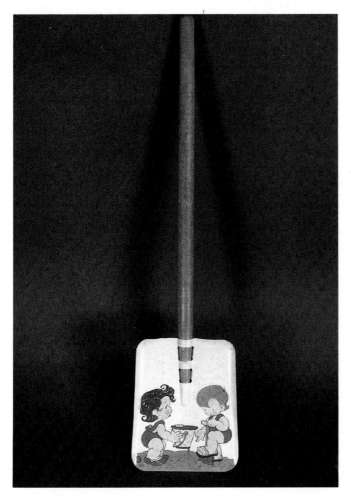

571 - SAND SHOVEL - 17¾″ x 4¼″. Metal litho shovel has painted wooden handle. c. 1950.

572- SAND PAIL AND SHOVEL - Pail. 6¼″ x 4½″; shovel: 8³/₈″ L. Metal litho cowboy and Indian motif sand pail comes with matching shovel. c. early 1950s.

573 - MUSIC BOX - 6″ H., 5½″ Dia. Cylindrical metal litho music box plays four notes when handle is turned. Original box is plain cardboard. c. 1948.

574 - TOE-JOE - 9½″ x 4½″ base, 16″ H. Acrobatic clown is molded plastic, wire and cloth. Metal litho stand. Mid-50s-late 60s.

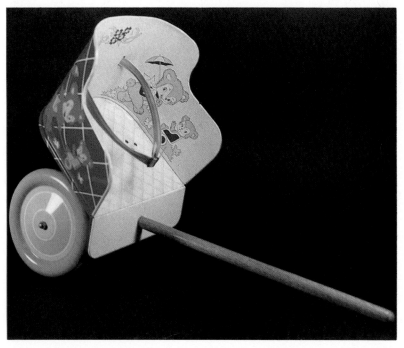

575 - TWO-WHEELED DOLL STROLLER - 7½″ x 9¼″ x 10¾″ H., 13″ handle. Metal litho seat and wheels, wooden handle. c. 1950.

576 - WATERING CAN - 8″ H. x 5″ Dia. Metal litho sprinkling can--one of many in several sizes and designs made by Ohio Art through the years. c. 1950.

577 - SPINNING TOP - 4¾″ Dia., 3¾″ H. One of many metal litho tops in various sizes made by Ohio Art. Identifying marks in this lithography appear hand lettered. c. 1950.

578 - SUNNYFIELD FARMS BARN - Base: 15″ x 8½″; 10½″ H. to roof peak. Metal litho barn with attached silo, sliding door and one open side. No interior lithography. Set came with plastic fence sections and 18 animals. c. 1950.

579A - MEADOW LANE FARM - 15¾″ x 9½″ x 12″ H. Metal litho barn has two-piece roof, no inside lithography. Set of 40 + pieces includes family figures, animals, fence sections, tractor and implements. (Head missing from boy figure.) c. 1960.

579B - MEADOW LANE FARM - Box is in shape of barn.

580 - SPRINGDALE FARM SET - Barn: 9″ x 9¼″ x 14″. 46-piece set includes: metal litho barn and corn crib, vinyl playmat, tractor and five implements, hay bale, livestock feeder, 16 animals, farm hand tools and blue plastic fence sections. c. late 1960s.

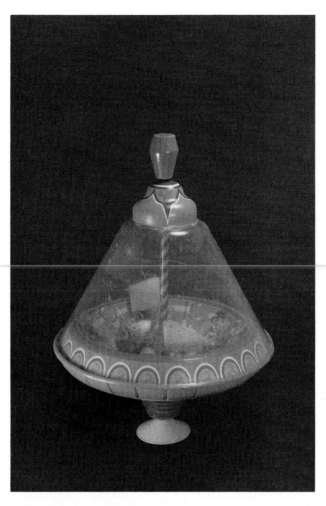

581 - SPIRAL SPINNING TOP - 8″ Dia., 11″ H. Metal litho and plastic top has two yellow paddles and eight plastic marbles inside which spin as top spins.

582 - SPIRAL TOP - 6½″ Dia., 6″ H. Metal litho spinning top has "Ten Little Indians" motif.

583 - METAL DRUM - 6″ Dia. Metal litho drum with metal heads has marching band around sides.

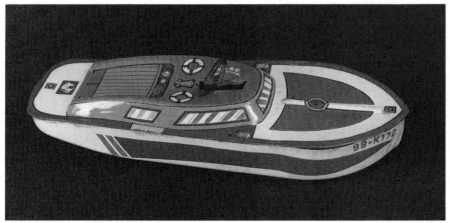

584 - SPEED BOAT - Propeller-driven metal litho boat. Winds up on top.

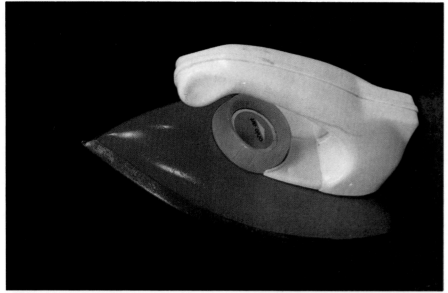

585 - PLAY IRON - Red metal iron has white plastic handle and yellow dial.

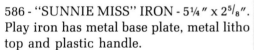

586 - "SUNNIE MISS" IRON - 5¼″ x 2⅝″. Play iron has metal base plate, metal litho top and plastic handle.

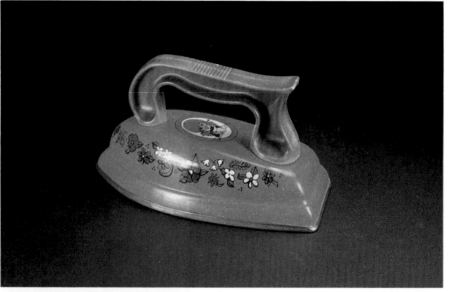

587 - MUSICAL COLOR T.V. - 9″ x 10″ x 4½″. Plastic case holds a picture paper roll mounted on music box mechanism. c. 1965.

588 - "THE HUMMER" TEA SET ASSORT-MENT - Different pictures appeared on this group. 1932.

589 - "FAIRY & FLORAL" - 4 place setting included 7½″ x 5½″ serving tray, 4 - 4″ plates (shown), 4 cups (shown) and saucers, creamer (shown at right), 2 handled sugar bowl and rounded teapot with lid. 1933-35.

590 - ITEM #19 (no name) - 15 pc. tea set included 4 rounded cups (same as in "Fairy & Floral" set), 4 saucers, 4 - 4″ plates (shown), rounded teapot and cover, and 5½″ x 7½″ tray. 1948-50.

591 - "MEXICAN BOYS" - 9 pc. tea set included 2 straight-sided cups, 2 saucers (shown), 2 - 4″ plates, straight-sided teapot (shown) with cover, and 5½″ x 7½″ tray. 1942-43; 1946-47.

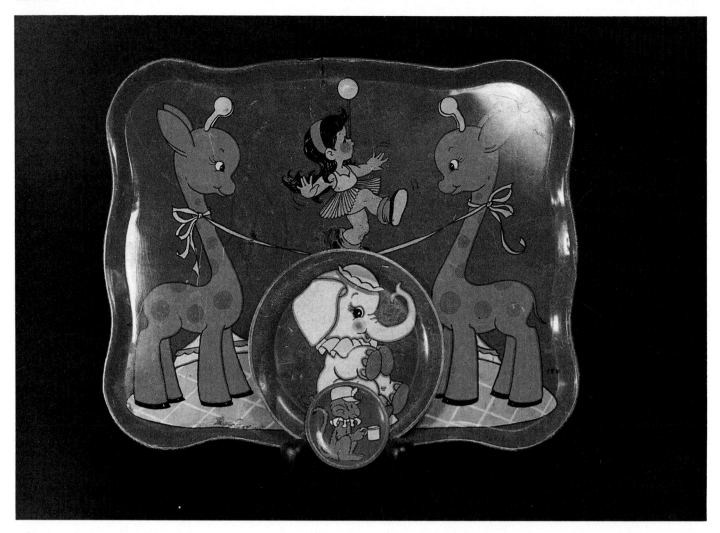

592 - ITEM #80; CIRCUS MOTIF - 31 pc. tea set included 6 rounded cups, 6 saucers, 6 butter plates (shown), 6 - 4″ plates (shown), handled dish with cover, straight-sided creamer (like teapot in "Mexican Boys" set), footed sugar bowl, rounded teapot with lid and an 8″ x 10″ tray. 1949.

593 - (No name - boy, girl & kitten motif) - At least 2 size sets were available in this pattern. The 7 pc. set included 2 straight-sided cups (shown); 2 saucers (shown); a straight-sided teapot (shown) and cover; and a 4″ plate from the larger set, which served as a tray. The 9 pc. set included all of the above plus another 4″ plate and a 5½″ x 7½″ tray. 1949.

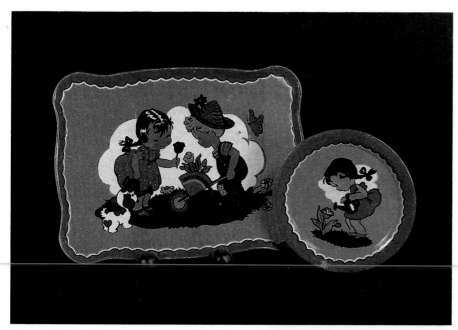

594 - (No name - girl with watering can motif) - 14 pc. set available in 1956 included 4 rounded cups, 4 saucers, 4 plates (shown), straight-sided teapot, and a 5½″ x 7½″ tray (shown). Cups, saucers and teapot show only the brown and white dog on yellow background with red edging. 1950-57.

595 - (No name - Bluebirds motif) - 8 pc. set included 2 rounded cups, 2 saucers, 2 plates, straight-sided teapot and 5½″ x 7½″ tray (shown). Bluebirds appear on all pieces. c. 1956.

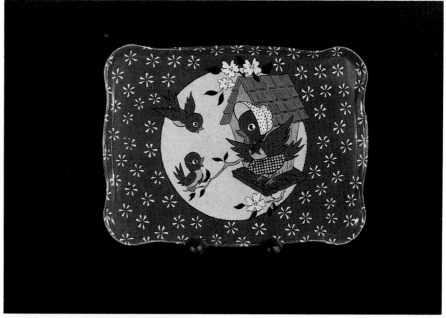

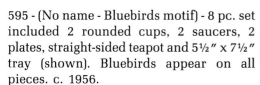

596 - "RED PLAID" TEA SET - A 20 pc. set included large straight-sided teapot, straight-sided creamer (same as "Mexican Boys" teapot), footed sugar bowl (shown), 4 cups (shown), 4 saucers (shown), 4 plates (shown), 4 butter plates (shown), and 8″ x 10″ tray (shown). c. 1956.

597 - Probably a "special" - No record available on this pattern. One of the larger sets--probably a 31 pc. set. Date unknown.

598 - Probably a "special" - No record available on the "Bunny Birthday Party" motif. Pieces suggest a 9 pc. set--2 straight-sided cups (shown), 2 saucers, 2 plates (shown), straight-sided teapot and lid, and 5½" x 7½" tray (shown). Appears to be from the 1940's.

PLASCO

599 - PLASCO ALICE IN WONDERLAND TEATIME DISHES - Cup: $1^7/_8''$ H.; box is $20^1/_2''$ x $14^1/_4''$. A 16-pc. tea set in three colors of brittle plastic. Teapot has an applied white plastic "Alice" medallion on one side. "Queen of Hearts" is in the center of each saucer. The 1952 version was 46-pc. set in either pink or blue which included napkins, cutlery and tea service for six. A smaller set with service for two was available for 98¢. Price in 1949 - $2.98.

PLAYTIME TOYS

600 - PLAYTIME TOYS RED IRON - 5"x 2¾" x 3½" H. Iron has metal base plate, red plastic body and black plastic handle. c. 1954.

PRESSMAN

601 - PRESSMAN TIDDLEDY WINKS - $6^5/_8''$ sq. box. Printed cardboard game and box has paper center cup and plastic playing pieces. c. 1946.

PLAYSKOOL

In the 1920s, an employee of the John Schroeder Lumber Company in Milwaukee, Wisconsin, originated the idea of manufacturing and marketing wooden toys that she had developed to use in the classroom when she was a teacher. By 1930, the Playskool Institute was producing around 40 items; and in 1935, the company became a division of Thorncraft, Inc. When Playskool Institute was bought by The Joseph Lumber Company in 1938, one of the first new employees hired was Manuel Fink. Robert Mayerthaler joined the company two years later, and the two men bought the firm a few years after that. Lincoln Logs, one of Playskool Mfg. Co.'s most popular and long-lived items, was brought into the line when the J. L. Wright Company merged with Playskool in 1943. Another merger which furthered the company's growth was that of Holgate toys in 1958. Playskool purchased South Bend Toy Mfg. Co. in 1960 and Halsam in 1962. Then in 1968, Playskool became a subsidiary of Milton-Bradley, well-known manufacturer of many games.

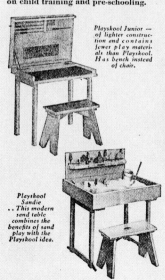
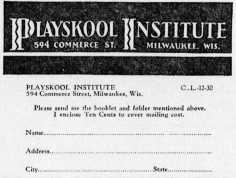

602X - December 1930 *Child Life* ad. Courtesy Bianca Hoekzema.

603 - PUSH-ALONG - ALL-WOODEN TOY - Figure spins around when toy is pushed. Courtesy Betty Jane Updike.

604 - CATERPILLAR PULL TOY - Wooden cylinders hooked together with wood strips and metal pins undulates across floor. c. 1951.

605 - COL-O-ROL WAGON - 12¾" L. x 9½" W. x 3½" H. Wooden wagon holds painted wooden cubes, cylinders and triangular blocks with center holes. Also painted wooden dowels. c. 1951.

606 - TWO-FIGURE LEVER TOY - When lever is hit with hammer, wooden figures are propelled upward to strike bell. (Hammer not shown.)

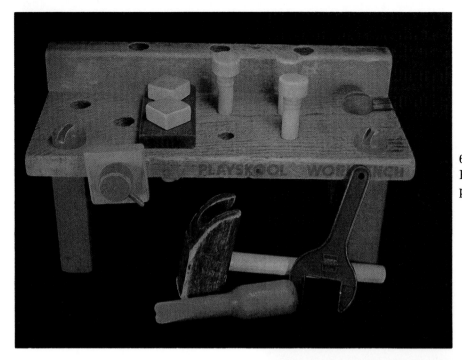

607 - WORKBENCH - 11½″ L. x 5¾″ H. Bench and all pieces are wooden except for plastic wrench. c. 1951.

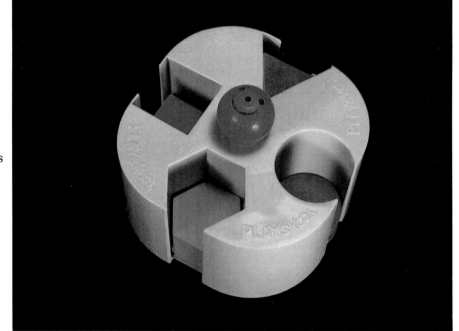

608 - SHAPE SORTER - Plastic base holds flat wooden shapes in stacks.

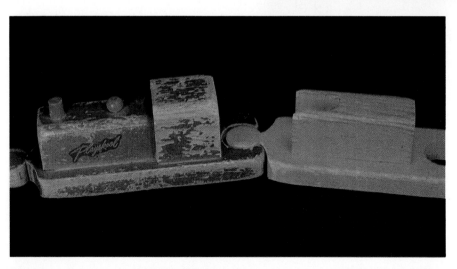

609 - WOODEN TRAIN - Blue engine: 7½″ L. Two pieces of a train of unknown size.

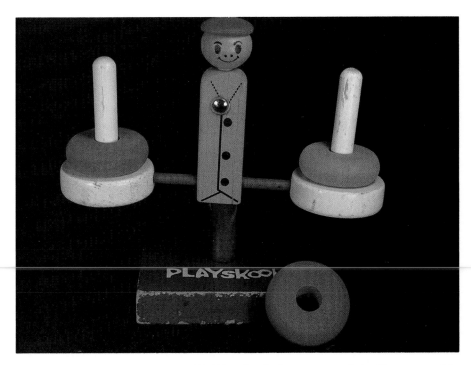

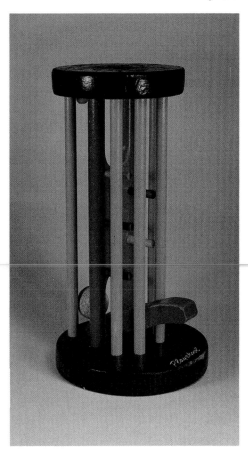

610 - BALANCE - 5″x 3″ x 8″ H. Wooden balance toy originally came with six rings.

611 - BALL & LEVER TOY - All wooden. Ball is propelled upward when lever is struck, and it falls down through a series of dowels.

612 - BALL & LEVER TOY - 10″ H. x 7″ W. All wooden toy similar to preceding one.

613 - STACKING RINGS - Bell rings as each wooden disc is put on the post.

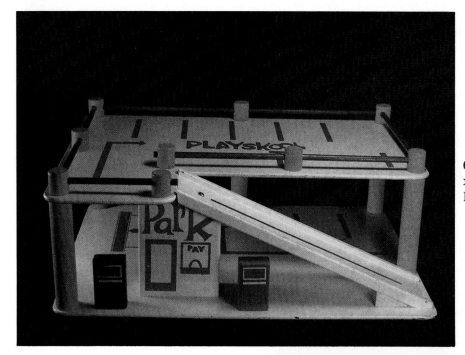

614 - PARKING GARAGE - 15¾″ x 11½″ x 6″ H. Constructed of wood and Masonite. Probably came with wooden cars.

615 - WOODEN TRAIN - Cars have hook and eye connectors. Only caboose is marked. Several color variations.

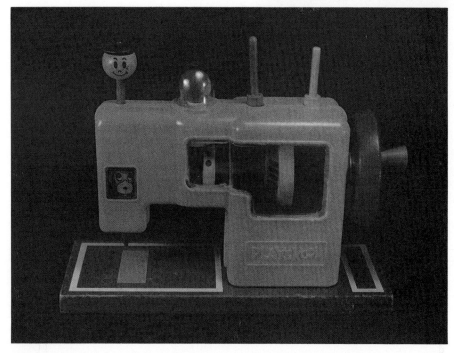

616 - SEWING MACHINE - Yellow plastic machine on wooden base. Wooden spindles and gears turn, bob up and down when handle is turned to "sew."

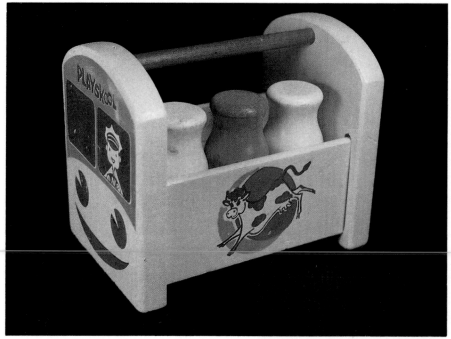

617 - MILK CARRIER - 6¼″ x 4¼″ x 5¼″ H. All painted wood. The complete toy included two more "white" milk bottles, one "chocolate," and a flat wooden wagon to set carrier on. c. 1963. Price in 1963 - $2.29.

618 - WALKER WAGON OF BLOCKS - 19″ L. x 8¼″ W. All wooden wagon had curved metal handle similar to wagon in following photo. Holds 20 wooden blocks. c. 1963. Price in 1963 - $3.74.

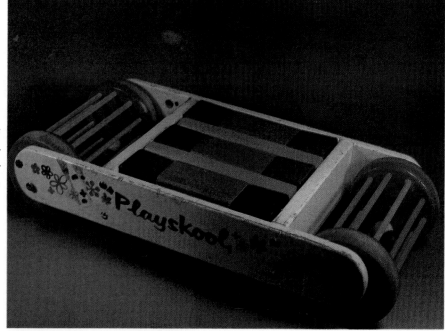

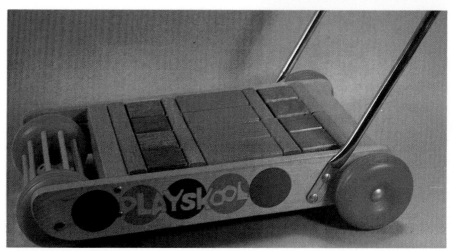

619 - WALKER WAGON OF BLOCKS - 18″ x 8″. A newer version of the preceding toy, this one has plastic "balloon" wheels and only one cylinder cage.

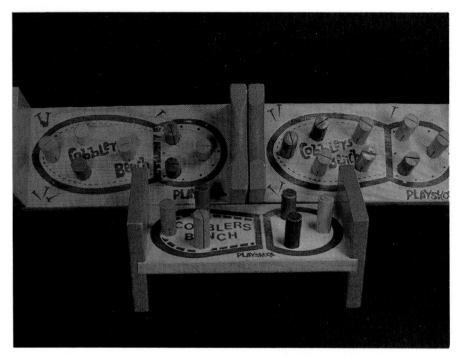

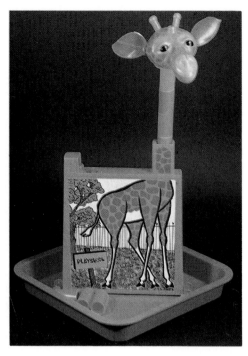

620 - COBBLER'S BENCH - Group of three pounding benches showing evolutionary changes. Bench top right is oldest; bottom, newest.

621 - LONG-NECKED GIRAFFE - 9¼″ sq. base. All plastic toy has paper lithos on two sides. Yellow and orange cylinders are inserted into hole on left, making neck longer and longer. (Orange vinyl ears and spinner missing.) c. 1971.

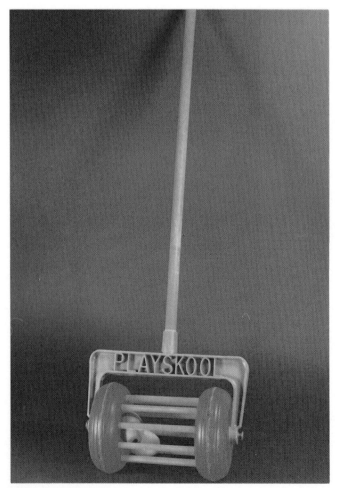

623 - APPLE RATTLE - 6¾″ x 4¼″. Plastic apple half has clear plastic top. Three wooden balls inside. Vinyl stem and leaf piece.

622 - RATTLE PUSH - 23½″ L. Combination wood and plastic.

624A and 624B - TRAVELLING PET HOSPITAL - Playset includes: blue plastic van/storage case; vinyl dog, puppies, cat, rabbit, bird and stethoscope; plastic food dish, instruments, stretcher, and two animal beds; veterinarian figure.

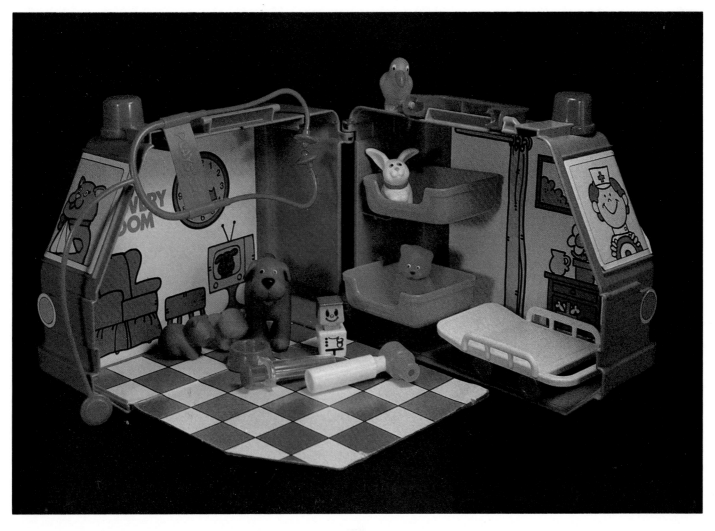

625 - VENDING MACHINE SHAPE SORTER - Plastic vending machine dispenses cubes, triangles and cylinders which are put back into their slots through holes in the top.

626 - LACING SHOE SHAPE SORTER - 8½″ L. x 6″ W. x 7″ H. Wooden and fibreboard shoe has plastic wheels. Wooden people fit into their corresponding window holes.

627 - CAPTAIN SEAGULL - Two-piece water toy. Seagull seated on life preserver float. When pushed down into water, wings raise and whistle inside bill cries like a gull.

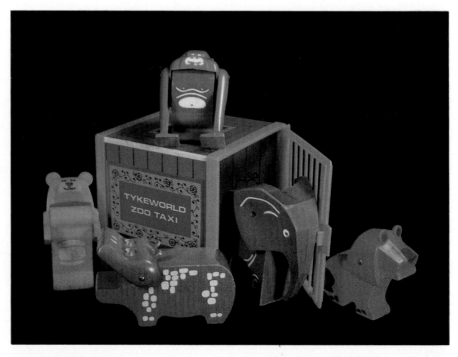

628 - TYKEWORLD ZOO - Hippo: 5″ L. Wooden block-bodied zoo animals have pin-jointed plastic heads. Cardboard and plastic cage may have had wheeled base originally.

629 - NESTING CUBES - Hollow plastic green cube holds smaller yellow one which holds white one with bell inside.

630 - CHIMING SCHOOL BELL - 7½″ H. All plastic bell has chiming mechanism inside.

631 - POUNDING BENCH - 11″ x 4¼″ x 6″ H. A particularly well-made version of the peg pounding bench. Shape of pegs prevents their coming out.

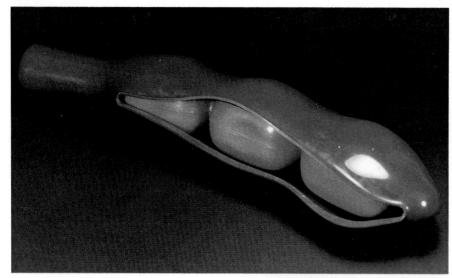

632 - PEAS IN A POD - Green vinyl pod holds three snap-together plastic "peas." c. 1973.

633 - ANIMALS AND LETTERS - 25 colored plastic animals recessed in back to hold the first letters of their names. c. 1973. Courtesy Tom Johnson.

634 - "THREE LITTLE PIGS" - 11" H. Two versions of the same toy. Pig with ribbon is from 1973, the other from 1974. Clothing panel has velcro fastener. Four-page cloth storybook inside.

635 - "BABY BEAR" - 11″ H. Another of the same type toy as preceding pigs showing book inside. c. 1974.

636 - CLEAN-UP TRUCK - 15″ x 6″ x 6½″ H. Five-piece set is all plastic. Driver is a brush, helper a dustpan White bucket with handle holds sponge and lifts out. Truck is not marked. c. 1974. Price in 1974 - $5.77.

637 - PLAY FRIENDS NATIONAL PARK - 33-piece playset includes: 2 flocked reversible islands, flocked 29½″ x 20½″ playmat, four camper figures with two backpacks, two-piece tree and tree stump, bear cave, beaver dam, ranger tower and ladder, Park Information booth, car, canoe, tent, Ranger with hat, campfire, bucket, and 24-pg. "National Park System" booklet. There are also nine animals with jointed parts, consisting of a rabbit, owl, deer, bear, eagle, squirrel, skunk, beaver and raccoon.

638 - TAKE APART JEEP - 9½" L. x 4" H. All plastic components with two wooden side pieces. (Came with combination wrench/screwdriver, not shown.) c. 1975. Original price, $4.94.

639 - STUFFED BUNNY BALL - 6" Dia. Plush ball has ears and feet for easy grabbing. c. 1976.

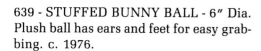

640 - DOG AND CAT IN A BARREL - Cylinder: 4" H. White plastic cylinder has cloth cat in one end and dog inside the other. Bell inside. c. 1976.

641 - McDONALD'S PLAYSET - Includes: 24″ x 27½″ vinyl playmat, main building, two passenger cars, sign base and sign, round yellow table, yellow whirl-around ride, six trays, three McDonald's employee figures, four customer figures. c. 1974.

642 - SESAME STREET NEIGHBOR-HOOD - Buildings made by fitting three sides into plastic roof and base pieces. Set includes: five buildings, playmat, and eight figures with stands: mail box, fire hydrant, phone booth, tree and street light. c. 1977.

643 - COOK 'N' SERVE GRILL - 9¼″ x 7¼″ x 4″ H. All plastic grill and utensils. Round food cards show raw food on one side, cooked on the other. (Fork and apron not shown.) c. 1977.

RICHARD SCARRY'S PUZZLETOWN SETS - Playsets featuring Richard Scarry's familiar characters. Besides those shown here were: Set B, "Huckle Cat's Family Cottage," and Set D, "Mayor Fox's Town Center."

644A - SET A - Dr. Lion's Medical Center playset includes: Dr. Lion, Nurse Nelly and Flossie, two-piece ambulance, stretcher, bed, two ramps, eight roof pieces, two bases, 11 woodboard pieces to make buildings.

644B - SET C - Farmer Alfalfa's Farm playset includes: Farmer Alfalfa, Mother Goat and Cow, truck, trailer, six roof pieces, silo top, three bases, two ramps and 42 woodboard pieces.

644C - SET E - Lowly Worm's Rail and Roadway playset includes: Lowly Worm, Engineer Fox and Conductor Dog, two-piece train, water tower, crossing gate, roadster, baggage cart, six straight and four curved track sections, one train track intersection, two ramps, eight roof pieces, two bases and 17 woodboard pieces.

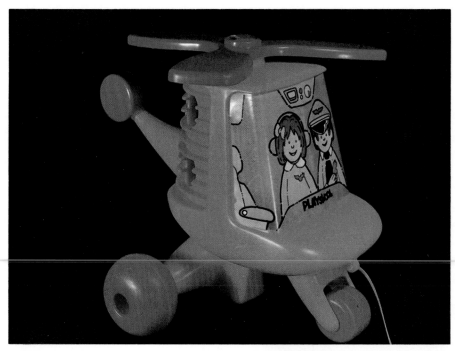

645 - COLOR GLOW COPTER - All plastic with paper litho windshield. c. 1977.

646 - BEAR SHAPE SORTER - Plastic shapes fit through corresponding holes in plastic bear. Squeaker in hat. 1978-present.

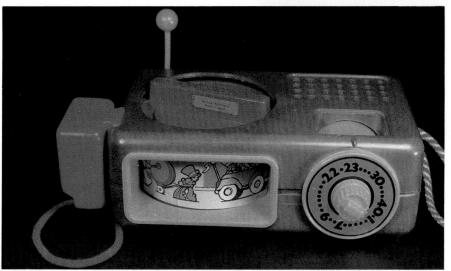

647 - MUSICAL BAND RADIO - All plastic with paper litho picture cylinder. Green handle winds music box. c. 1977.

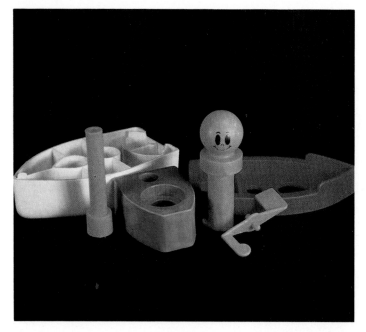

648A - TAKE APART TUGBOAT - 5″ x 3½″ H. Figure is the key piece--turning it makes the others come apart. Other vehicles were available.

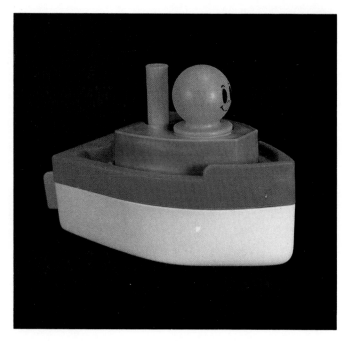

648B - TAKE APART TUGBOAT

649 - STUFFED BEAR RATTLE - 6½″ x 8″. Pockets on back of arms make it a finger puppet. c. 1978.

650 - ALPHIE - Battery-operated question-and-answer robot comes with variety of cards and games. c. 1978-present. (New model in 1983.)

651 - BEAR WAGON - Four-piece plastic stacking bear sits on blue plastic wagon.

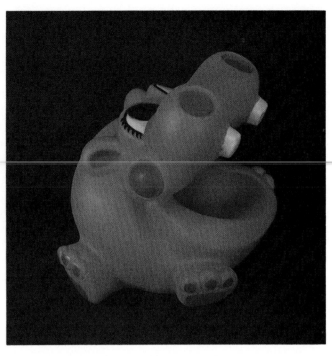

652 - HIPPO - 4″ H. Vinyl infant toy. c. 1979.

653 - APPLE TURNOVER - 8¼″ x 6″ x 6″ H. (with apple.) Hollow plastic apple turns over and over on plastic roller base. c. 1979-present.

654 - BEE RATTLE - 4½″ x 4¼″. Plastic balls inside wing "hide" in body, reappear in other wing.

655 - SQUEAKER PETS - Fabric animals have squeakers inside. Owl: 1977-present. Dog and frog: 1978-present.

656 - GILLIGAN'S FLOATING ISLAND - Playset can be used on land or water and includes: main island, 2-pc. hut, 2-pc. "sprinkler" palm tree, boat, raft, treasure chest, anchor and flag, and three vinyl figures: Skipper, Gilligan and Mary Ann. 1980-present.

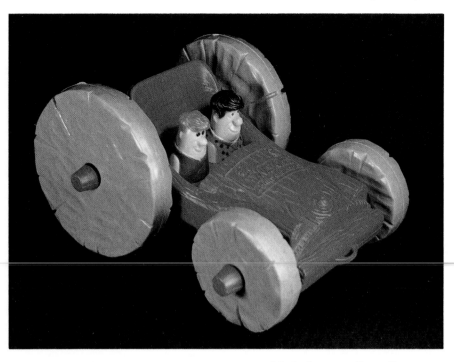

658 - FLINTSTONE CAR - 9¼″ L. x 5″ H. Molded plastic pull toy flips over. Fred and Barney on one side; Pebbles and Bam-Bam on the other. c. 1976.

657 - TINKERTOY - This set of the well-known Tinkertoy was made by Questor.

QUESTOR

659 - LADYBUG - Friction toy has red plastic shell with painted metal dome underneath which revolves. Also available was a green turtle.

660 - CAMP KAMP - Heavy flexible vinyl playset featuring Charles Schultz' "Peanuts" characters.

REMPEL

662 - SANTA CLAUS - 10½″ H. Latex rubber Santa squeaker toy. 1950s.

661 - FRISKEY, THE RIDE 'EM COWBOY STICK - 36″ stick. Riding stick has rubber horse head and front legs on one end, two wheels on the other. c. 1958. Courtesy Jessie Hanson.

663 - SQUEAKER SQUEEZE TOYS - Hobo: 6¾″ H: Three of Rempel Enterprise's beautiful rubber figures. Two have the high gloss characteristic of many of their toys. Perhaps their most familiar toy is "Froggie, the Gremlin" which sticks out his tongue when squeezed. Since rubber disintegrates relatively quickly, these toys are rarely found in excellent condition. c. 1955.

SCHOENHUT

664Xa and 664Xb - Shoenhut ad from 1930 *Child Life*. Courtesy Bianca Hoekzema.

665X - November 1954 magazine ad.

SCHOENHUT

666A, 666B and 666C - Schoenhut TUNES FROM MOTHER GOOSE. c. 1940. Courtesy Jean Couch. Photo by Jerry Couch.

STRUCTO

668 - STRUCTO "PLAYMATE GUIDANCE" SCHOOL BUS - 12″ x 4″ x 5½″ H. Brittle plastic bus with red plastic wheels is hinged at the back and opens from the front. Four plastic block holders snap into the sides, and each holds three plain wooden blocks. Clear plastic windshield. c. 1950.

SPALDING

667 - SPALDING TINKERTOY - This set of Tinkertoys was manufactured by Spalding Bros.

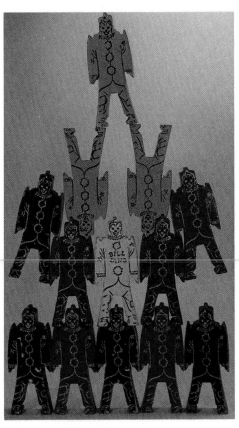

STROMBECKER

669 - STROMBECKER BILL-DING CLOWNS - 4½″ H. Set of 14 wooden clowns that fit together in many configurations. Only one clown, the white one, is marked "Bill-Ding" in each set. Set came with toss rings and a booklet describing games to play with the clowns. 1940s-1950s.

TUDOR

671 - TUDOR WALKIE-TALKIE RADIO PHONE - Metal litho reproduction of a portable radio set used in World War II. Courtesy John Courtwright.

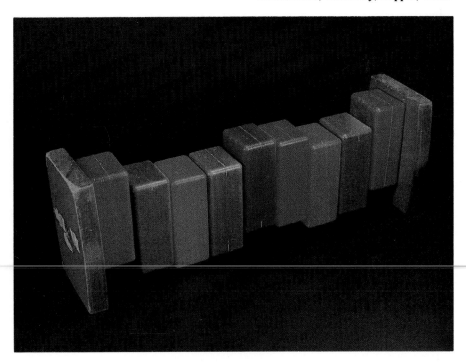

TINKERTOY

670 - TINKERTOY POUND-A-BLOCK - 15″ x 5″ H. Wood and vinyl pounding toy made by one of the manufacturers of Tinkertoys.

TOPPER

672 - TOPPER WALKING LETTERS - Part of a toy shown in No. 673X magazine ad on following page. c. 1971.

For the first time, educational playthings based on your child's favorite TV series.

1. Ernie Hand Puppet—Almost any child can operate his arms and mouth.

2. Bert Hand Puppet—Ernie's inseparable buddy. Just like Ernie.

3. Cookie Monster Hand Puppet—His arms and mouth move, and you can feed him cookies.

4. Oscar Hand Puppet—The world's most lovable "Grouch."

5. Big Bird—He's almost 19 inches tall. Bend him, pose him in all sorts of positions. Make his beak move and his wings flap.

6. Spell-A-Phone—"Dial" a word, and the "word" will talk to you. Dial characters from Sesame Street, too. A whole new way to teach youngsters to spell.

7. Walking Letters—Letters actually "walk" down the ramp as you spell the word. Get it right, and Big Bird pops up to congratulate you. Wrong? The letters fall down!

8. Sherlock Hemlock Magic Puzzles—Complete with the Magic Looking Glass to discover hidden answers, letters, and numbers. The real fun starts after you put it together.

Each of above Sesame Street toys is guaranteed in writing for one year from date of purchase against defective materials and workmanship. This educational product was developed in close

cooperation with the producers, researchers and educational advisors of the Children's Television Workshop, creators of the Sesame Street television series.

This product is intended to further the instructional goals of Sesame Street, but it has independent educational value and children do not have to watch the television show to benefit from it.

Workshop revenues from this product will be used to help support Sesame Street and other C.T.W. educational projects. Big Bird and the Muppets are Jim Henson creations.

*Trademark of C.T.W. ©1971 Children's Television Workshop. Muppets © Muppets, Inc. Products of Educational Toys, Inc., a subsidiary of TOPPER CORPORATION
© 1971, Topper Corp

673X - Topper Sesame Street ad from 1971.

674 - TOPPER BIG BIRD - 18½″ H. Stuffed plush figure has hard plastic eyes and feet, flexible vinyl beak and legs and felt "hands." Hole in back of head to make beak move; poseable. c. 1971.

TOMY

Strictly speaking, this is a Japanese company with headquarters in Carson, California. Begun in a California garage in 1973, this company is an infant in the toy field. The fine design and workmanship employed by Tomy insures their place in future toy collections.

675 - PASS THE NUTS - 10½″ H. x 8¼″ W. By pressing the proper level, the "nut" is passed upward and into the bird nest. c. 1974.

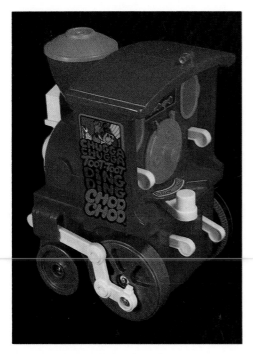

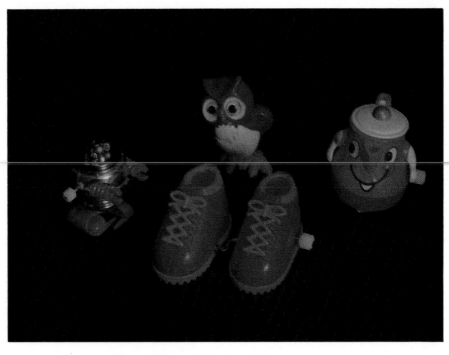

676 - CHUGGA CHUGGA TOOT TOOT DING DING CHOO CHOO - 6″ x 6″ x 9″ H. Battery-operated plastic locomotive has levers to control on/off, stop/go, slow/fast, bell and whistle. A feast of sound and motion! c. 1979.

677 - A few of Tomy's little wind-up critters. c. 1977.

678 - ANSWER CLOCK - 9¾″ H. x 7″ W. All-plastic toy for teaching time. Pressing red buttons opens owl's eyes, showing hour and minutes. c. 1975.

679 - TUNEYVILLE PLAYER PIANO - 8½″ H. Battery-operated plastic piano comes with four plastic records and color-coded sheet music. (Also available is the "Tuneyville Choo-Choo"--a white plastic locomotive which operates on batteries and uses larger records.) c. 1978.

TONKA

Best known for its metal vehicles in all sizes, Tonka also made a preschool line.

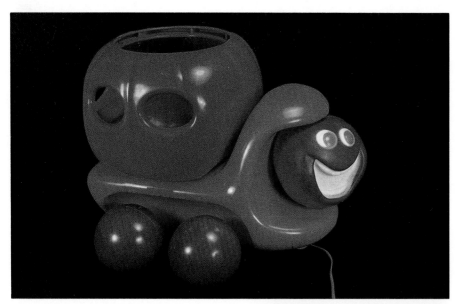

680A, 680B and 680C - TONKA TOD-DLERS PULL TOYS - A group of molded plastic toys in various shapes. Toys in these photos are missing the tops and accessories that came with each one.

681 - PEOPLE - Hard plastic egg-shaped figures have painted clothes and three different faces. hair is a separate piece which turns to show each face. These figures go in the "Toddler" vehicles.

TOWNER TOY

682 - TOWNER TOY FIRE ENGINE - Mallet strikes bell when wooden hook and ladder truck is pulled. Courtesy of Betty Jane Updike.

THE TOY TINKERS

Tinkertoys were invented by a tombstone cutter named Charles H. Pajeau and were introduced in 1914. The toy industry rejected Pajeau's building sets almost unanimously, but the public didn't! Displays of his toys in store windows caused traffic jams, and as many as 50 gross of the sets were sold at one store in one day. Along with Henry Keuls and Robert Pettit, his two original partners, Pajeau expanded his manufacturing facilities over the next few years. They added other toys to their line--wooden bead figures strung with springs, and pull toys. When Pajeau died in 1952, the Tinkertoy line was purchased by the sporting goods firm, A. G. Spalding & Bros., Inc. This company was a division of Questor. In 1955, colored parts were added; in 1964, cardboard pieces were replaced by plastic ones; and in 1965, motorized kits were introduced. In January of 1978, Gabriel Industries acquired Tinkertoys and the entire Child Guidance line of toys from Questor. In August of that same year, Gabriel became part of C.B.S., Inc.

683 - TINKERTOY SET - Well-known Tinkertoy building set. Box is 12¼" H., 3" Dia. c. 1930.

684 - SWIMMER - This wooden pull toy is supported by a metal base structure. Arms "swim" and legs "kick" as it is pulled. c. 1930. Courtesy of Betty Barry.

685 - PONY TINKER - 8″ L. x 6½″ H. Rider bobs up and down when toy is pulled. Courtesy of Betty Jane Updike. c. 1930.

686 - PUPPY TINKER - 6″ L. x 3¾″ H. Small dog made with painted wooden beads. Springs run from head through body pieces into tail, making a variety of positions possible. Black felt ears. c. 1940.

TUPPERWARE

The familiar manufacturer of vinyl kitchen equipment also makes a line of "Tupper Toys."

687 - BUILD-O-FUN - Box: 13⅝″ x 3¼″. Four basic plastic shapes slide together to build objects. c. 1965.

688 - KUP-L-UPS - Molded plastic shapes snap together to form many objects. Wheels and hubcaps included. c. 1969. Courtesy of Tom Johnson.

689 - SNAP TOGETHER BLOCKS - Hollow-plastic blocks snap open diagonally. Each block holds a solid green plastic figure whose name begins with the letter on the block. Blocks also snap together to form geometric designs, buildings, etc.

690 - SHAPE SORTER BALL - Two-piece plastic "ball" comes with ten plastic shapes to fit through corresponding holes.

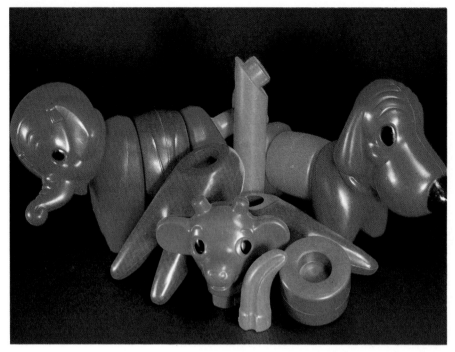

691 - ZOO-IT-YOURSELF - Multi-colored interlocking plastic head, leg, body, neck and tail sections mix or match to create zany animals or dog, elephant and giraffe.

TWINZY TOYS

692X - TWINZY TOYS ad from 1930 *Child Life*. Courtesy of Bianca Hoekzema.

Twinzy Toys

The NEW TWINZY PULL TOYS are here. Soft toys on wheels, combining the action in which children delight with the lovable life like feeling of a stuffed toy. Pictured at the left is the nation's favored DOG, the wired haired terrier. And who wouldn't want this grey maltese KITTEN? This bright colored ELEPHANT will follow you wherever you go. Then there is a yellow DUCK, a RABBIT and a cute little GIRL and BOY. All can be yours. Ask your dealer or send 50c for each toy. If you live west of the Rockies or in Canada, add 10c extra for each toy.

PULL DOG

PULL ELEPHANT

PULL CAT

TWINZY TOYS ARE DESIGNED BY TWINS

Ask SANTA CLAUS for TWINZY TOYS

- -

TWINZY TOY CO.   **Battle Creek, Mich.**

I enclose $........ for following TWINZY TOYS........

....

Name ....

City ....

State ....

JERRY GIRAFFE

$1.00 each

SCOTTY

$1.00 each

UNIQUE ART

693 - UNIQUE ART "CAPITOL HILL RACER" - Wind-up metal litho toy race car runs up hill, backs down, up, etc. c. 1935. Courtesy of Jim Yeager.

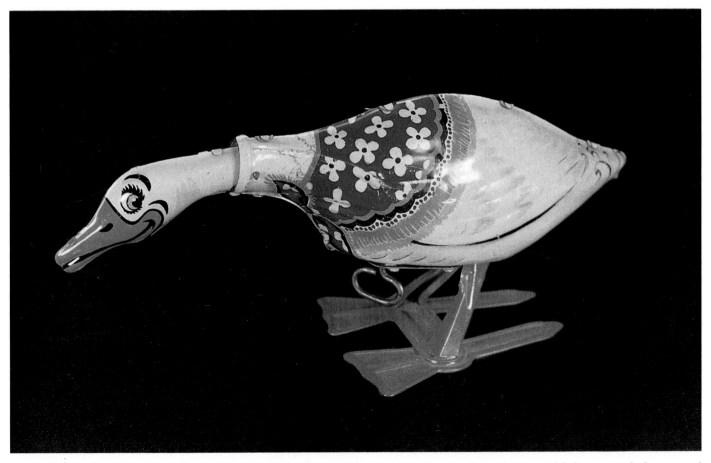

694 - UNIQUE ART "GERTIE THE GALLOPING GOOSE" - 9″ L. x 5½″ H.. Wind-up metal litho goose bobs up and down, "pecking" food. c. 1940.

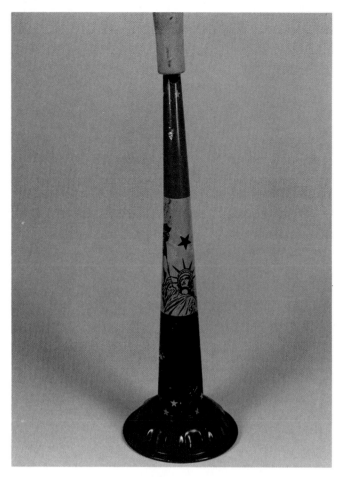

U.S. METAL TOY

695 - U.S. METAL TOY LIBERTY HORN - 10½" H. metal litho horn has combination metal and wood mouthpiece. Found wrapped in a V-Mail aerogram. Mid-1940s.

697 - U.S. METAL TOY SAND PAIL - 8" H. handle. Metal litho bucket.

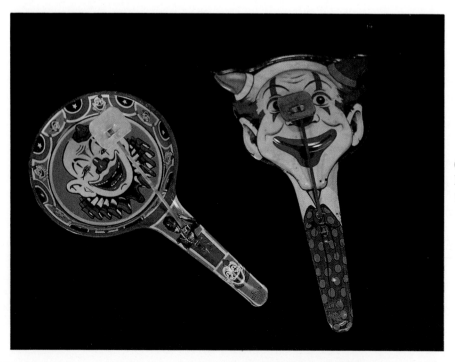

696 - U.S. METAL TOY CLOWN NOISEMAKERS - 8" L. metal litho noisemakers have metal clappers.

WESTERN STAMPING CO.

698 - WESTERN STAMPING CO. "TOM THUMB" CASH REGISTER - Steel cash registers came in red, green, pink or black. Earlier ones had metal cash drawers; later ones were plastic. Packet of play money and "Thank You" card came with it. 1950s and 60s.

WILSON

699 - WILSON SANTA "WALKIE" - 4¼″ H. slant board walker made from an old string cone. Wooden head with painted face, wooden legs and feet, crepe paper hat and chenille trim. c. late 1940s.

WOLVERINE

The Wolverine Supply & Mfg. Co. was founded in 1903 and incorporated in 1906 by Benjamin F. Bain. The first toys made by the company were tools for a sand toy that they had contracted to make for another manufacturer. Wolverine entered the toy field because the manufacturer who had ordered the tools went out of business, leaving them with all the sand toys. By 1913, Wolverine's line of sand toys, mechanical and gravity-action toys was being sold in most major department stores. James Lehren, sole salesman for the company for six years, and Joseph Schmitt, who was involved in factory operations, became president and vice president of the company when Mr. Bain died in 1926. Wolverine began making girls' housekeeping toys and action games in the 1920s as well as expanding their existing line. Toy production resumed after World War II, and Wolverine introduced Rite-Hite kitchen appliances in 1959. The name of the company was changed to Wolverine Toy Company in 1962; and in 1968, Wolverine was acquired by Spang and Co. of Butler, Pennsylvania. Since the factory in Pittsburgh was a series of antiquated buildings, one of Spang's first priorities was to update the facilities. A new plant was built in Booneville, Arkansas, and the company moved there at the end of 1970.

700 - JOLLY JUGGLER - 7″ x 3½″ x 12½″ H. Metal litho motion toy. The juggler holds a magnet which picks up "little helpers on magnets" and carries each one from chute to ground. Action continues as long as the magnet figures are replaced in the chute. c. 1930.

701 - SPRINKLING CAN - 9½″ H. x 5″ Dia. Metal litho sprinkling can has figures in bas relief.

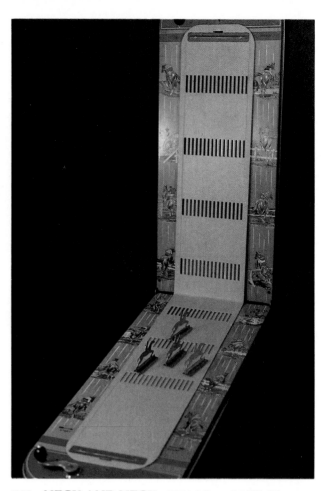

702 - NECK AND NECK - 36½″ L. x 8″ W. Horses: 2″ L. Metal litho track is hinged in the center for storing. Piece of heavy yellow paper is attached to bars at both ends and vibrates when handle is turned, causing the four metal horses to advance down the track. (Track is laid flat for play.)

703 - JOCKO PINBALL MARBLE GAME - 13″ x 7″. Metal litho back, clear plastic front. c. 1975.

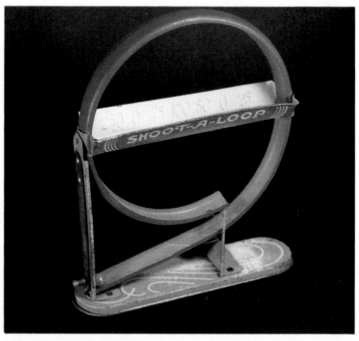

704 - SHOOT-A-LOOP - 9″ x 2¼″ x 8″ H. Metal litho spiral marble game. c. 1950.

705 - SKI JUMPER - Jump: 25¾″ L. x 4¾″ W. x 5″ H. Paper litho covered wooden skier rides on metal skis with four wheels. Metal ski poles and metal litho ski jump. When skier trips catch at bottom, spring-loaded platform throws him into the air. After doing a complete somersault over a bar, he lands on his wheels and rolls across the floor. (Poles and bar missing.) c. 1939. Price in 1939 - $1.00.

706 - SULKY RACER - 9″x 4″ x 5″ H. Plastic wind-up toy. c. 1951. Price in 1951 - $1.98.

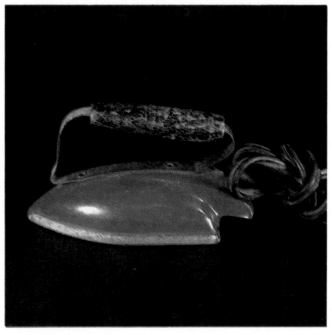

707 - SPOT SHOT - 12½″ L. x 5″ W. x 2¾″ H. Metal litho marble game. c. 1937.

708 - SUNNY SUZY ELECTRIC IRON - 5¼″ x 2½″ x 3¾″ H. c. 1940.

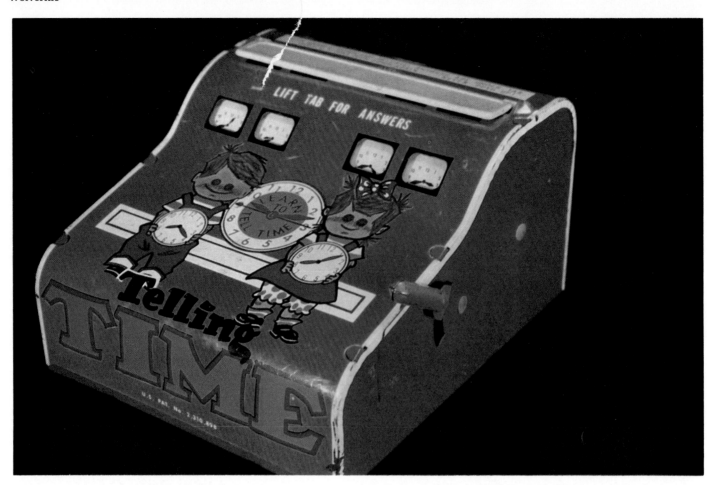

709 - TELLING TIME - 7″ x 6″ x 4″ H.. Metal litho time-teaching toy with plastic top panel.

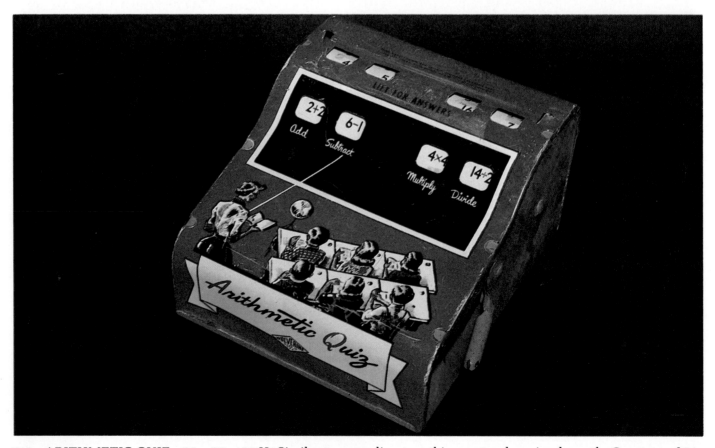

710 - ARITHMETIC QUIZ - 7″ x 6″ x 4″ H. Similar to preceding toy, this one teaches simple math. Courtesy of Liz Robertson.

J. L. WRIGHT, INC.

John Lloyd Wright, son of Frank Lloyd Wright, designed and developed "Lincoln Logs" in 1916. His idea for the building sets came when he was with his father in Tokyo and saw the construction techniques used in the earthquake-proof Imperial Hotel as it was being built. The Wright Company continued to manufacture "Lincoln Logs" until it merged with Playskool in 1943. "Lincoln Logs" have been one of Playskool's most popular toys ever since.

711 - LINCOLN LOGS - c. 1940. This early set of "Lincoln Logs" was found in the wooden box with side hinges that is pictured. Whether it is original or not is uncertain, but the pieces are a good fit. The front panel from the original cardboard box was inside along with the design book. The name "Lincoln Logs" was registered August 28, 1923, and the design book pictured was copyrighted in 1937. A "single set" consisted of 56 pieces, a "double set" 112 pieces, and a "complete set," 174 pieces. "Lincoln Log Timbers," square instead of round, were also available in three sets which sold for $1.00, $2.00 and $4.00. Set #50, "The Early American Fort Set," sold for $5.00 and included four soldiers of 1812, six Pottawotomie Indians (all metal), a powder house, flagpole and flag, and a settlers' cabin. Set #40, "The Fort Dearborn Construction Set," sold for $3.00 and did not contain the figures, powder house or settlers' cabin. Set #50CI, "The Settlers' Cabin," which sold for $1.00, came with two Indians, two cowboys and two pioneers. Other sets then available were: Set #71: Lincolnville RR Station and Five Figures which included Redcap, Engineer, Conductor, Passenger and Messenger Boy. Price, $1.00.; Set #80: The same five figures from set #71 PLUS Policeman and another Passenger. Price, 50¢.; Set #60: Barnyard Set. Includes a wooden barn, four sections of red and green fence and 11 figures: tree, horse, four pigs, cow, two sheep, farmer and wife. Price, $2.00; Set #70: Six figures only: farmer, sheep, horse, cow and two pigs. Price. 50¢.; Set #140: Twelve figures including: two trees, four pigs, cow, two sheep, a horse, farmer and wife. Price, $1.00.

712 - J. L. WRIGHT "MAKIT TOY" - An obvious copy of Tinkertoy. c. 1945.

WYANDOTTE

713 - WYANDOTTE DUST PAN - 7½″ x 6¼″. Painted steel dust pan.

714 - WYANDOTTE S. S. AMERICA - 7″ x 2″ x 2¼″ H. Metal litho ocean liner on four metal wheels. c. 1930s.

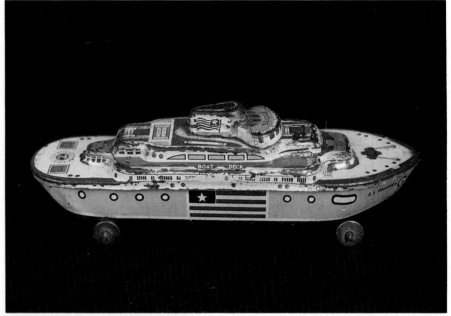

715 - WYANDOTTE LAYING HEN - 8″ x 5″ x 7″ H. Metal litho hen lays "eggs" when she is pushed down. c. 1940.

WHATSITS AND WHOOSITS

This is a group of pictures of toys that I haven't been able to identify in one way or another. Do you know what they are, who made them, and when they were produced?

716 - THREE BEARS RATTLES - Brittle plastic rattles. Courtesy Candy Bohn.

717 - JOHNNYVILLE BLOCKS - Painted embosed wooden blocks are 1¼″ cubes. Original set sold by F.A.O. Schwarz in 1939 included patterns shown here as well as triangular blocks, a wooden car and four turned-wood trees. c. 1939. Price in 1939 - $2.00. Halsam, maybe?

718 - TRIANGULAR ABACUS AND NUMBERS - 9½″ x 4⅞″. All wooden toy.

257

719 - GREEN IRON - 6½″ L. Lightweight enameled metal.

720 - SNOW WHITE CHALK CARNIVAL FIGURE - 14″ H. A nice example of chalk carnival art.

721 - BOY AND DOG CHALK CARNIVAL FIGURES - Boy: 15″ H. Dog: 3¼″ H. Dog is from the old Kansas City, Missouri, "Fairyland" Amusement Park and is dated August 15, 1954.

722 - LITTLE ORPHAN ANNIE STOVE - 8″x 4¼″ x 7¼″. Familiar stove came in several sizes.

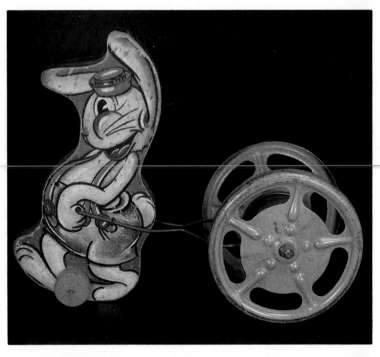

723 - RABBIT BELL PULL TOY - 10″ L. x 8″ H. Paper litho covered wooden rabbit is an Oswald look-alike.

724 - THREE-WHEELED CLOWN CAR - 3″ x 4¼″ H. Painted wooden car and clown head; plastic "eye" headlights.

725 - "GIRAFFE" CAR - 5½″ x 5″ H. Painted wooden vehicle probably had a triangular based giraffe that fit into the "back seat."

726 - VEGETABLE TRUCK - 7″ x 3″ H. Brittle plastic truck from early 1950s has separate plastic scale.

727 - BRITTLE PLASTIC WHISTLES - 4″ x 2½″ Locomotive sounds like a train whistle; 3″ x 1″ fire engine makes siren sound.

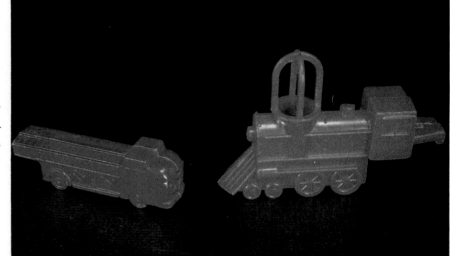

728 - BALLS AND BLOCKS - Heavy solid plastic balls and cubes with hemispherical depressions on two sides can be stacked in many ways.

729 - MANIPULATIVE ANIMAL PUZZLE - Colored arcs of a Bakelite-type material are joined by metal rivets. Wooden wheels. Many configurations are possible.

730 - PEOPLE BLOCKS - 1¼″ sq. x 1½″ H. Cylinders: 1⁷/₈″ L. Interchangeable paper litho covered wooden heads and bodies.

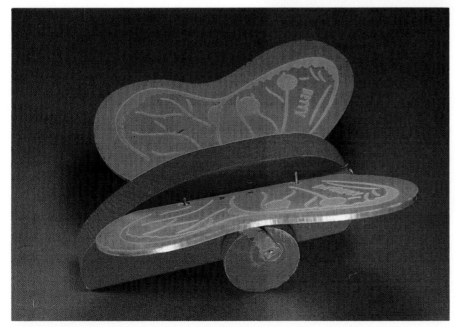

731 - BETTY BUTTERFLY - 8″ x 8½″ x 3″ H. Painted wooden pull toy flaps wings when pulled.

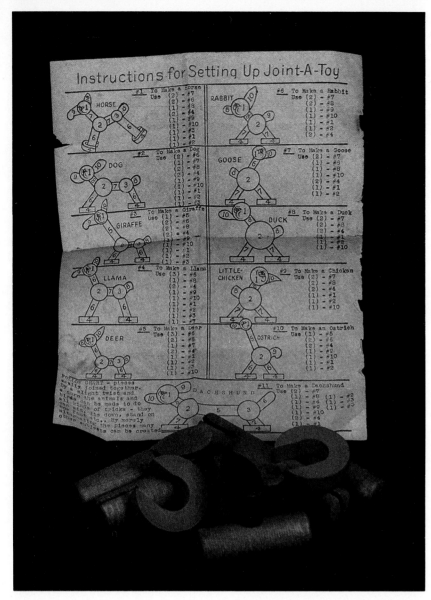

732 - JOINT-A-TOY - An incomplete set of colored wooden pieces which fit together to form various animals. c. 1940.

733 - FLAT IRONS - Small one: 2½" L.; large: 3¼" L. the smaller iron is all cast and unmarked. The larger one has a wooden handle and is marked "Dover, U.S.A." c. 1932. Courtesy of and photographed by Kathryn Fain.

734 - DOEPKE CLOWN - 9″ x 3″ x 7½″. Part of this painted wooden toy is missing. What is it? What did it do?

735 - PAINTED WOODEN CLOWN - 12½″ H. Part of a bowling set?

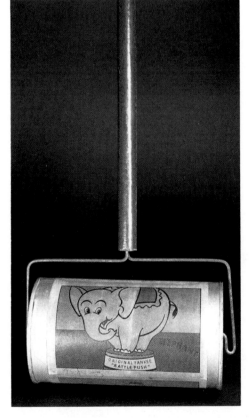

736 - ORIGINAL YANKEE RATTLE PUSH - Metal roller: 6″, x 3½″ Dia.; overall height, 24½″. Paper litho strip around metal cylinder; wire bracket wooden handle. Ink stamp under elephant says "selling price;" "75¢" has been written on with pencil.

737 - OLD WOODEN PEG POUNDING BENCH - This example of the familiar toy has an oak top.

PRICE LIST

Prices are listed for toys in "good" to "very good" condition, unless otherwise noted. S.A. designates "still available;" M.I.B., "mint in box;" M.I.P., "mint in package."

Several factors have influenced the changes in toy values since this book was first printed. The most significant changes will be found in older Fisher-Price, specific Marx and all Kenner "Star War" toys.

Photo Number	Price
1	$12.00-15.00
2X	Any of the four pull toys shown, each...$75.00-100.00
3	$8.00
4	$6.00
5X	These prices MIB or MIP only:
	Deluxe Doll-E Bath...$15.00
	Doll-E-Do Dish..$12.00-15.00
	Doll-E-Bed.....$10.00-12.00
	Doll-E-Nursette....$6.00-8.00
	Doll-E-Nurser...$25.00-30.00
	Doll-E-Crib.....$20.00-25.00
	Doll-E-Feeder...$30.00-35.00
	Doll-E-Hichair..$10.00-12.00
6	$10.00
7	$7.50
8	$15.00-20.00
9	$8.00
10	$8.00
11	$10.00
12	$6.00
13	$30.00-35.00
14	$12.00-15.00
15	S.A.
16X	Catalog ad
17	$27.00-33.00
18	$35.00-40.00
19	$15.00-18.00
20	$30.00-35.00
21	$12.00-15.00
22	$8.50
23	$20.00-22.50
24	$6.00-8.00
25	$25.00-30.00
26	$10.00-12.00
27	$6.00-7.00
28	$5.00-7.00
29	$8.00-10.00
30	$4.00-6.00
31	$1.50-2.00
32	$15.00-18.00
33	$10.00-12.50
34	$3.00
35	each $2.50
36	$30.00-35.00
37	entire set $12.00-15.00
38	$6.00-8.00
39	$15.00-18.00
40	$22.00-28.00
41X	Electric Ranges:
	B24..........$75.00-85.00
	B23........$200.00-240.00
	B26........$100.00-130.00
42	$6.00-8.00
43	$125.00-150.00
44X	Bunny Scoot....$125.00-150.00
	Drummer Bear...$130.00-160.00
45X	Granny Doodle...$140.00-175.00
	Doctor Doodle...$140.00-175.00
46X	Barky Puppy.....$115.00-140.00
	Lookee Monk...$115.00-140.00

Photo Number	Price
47X	Go 'N' Back:
	Mule.......$175.00-225.00
48X	Bruno......$175.00-225.00
	Jumbo......$175.00-225.00
49X	$125.00-150.00
50X	Woodsey-Wee Zoo$100.00-125.00
	Woodsey-Wee Pets$100.00-125.00
51X	Dizzy Dino.......$50.00-55.00
	Stoopy Storky.....$50.00-55.00
52X	Lofty Lizzy.......$50.00-55.00
	Tailspin Tabby....$30.00-35.00
53	$28.00-30.00
54	$25.00-28.00
55	$8.00-10.00
56	$20.00-25.00
57	Each toy in set....$15.00-20.00
58	$20.00-25.00
59	$3.00-4.00
60	$5.00-6.00
61	$10.00-12.00
62	$5.00-6.00
63	$4.00-5.00
64	$17.00-20.00
65	$4.00-6.00
66	$3.00-4.00
67	$15.00-17.00
68	$8.00-12.00
69	$8.00-10.00
70	MIB $60.00-65.00
71	complete $8.00-10.00
72	$20.00-25.00
73	$3.00-5.00
74	$20.00-25.00
75	$6.00-8.00
76	$10.00-12.00
77	$6.00-8.00
78	S.A.
79	S.A.
80	$40.00-45.00
81	$5.00-6.00
82	$2.00-4.00
83	complete $8.00-10.00
84	$15.00-20.00
85	$6.00-8.00
86	$10.00-15.00
87	complete $12.00-15.00
88	$3.00-5.00
89	$3.00-5.00
90	$1.00-3.00
91	$6.00-8.00
92	$1.00-3.00
93	$6.00-8.00
94	$6.00-8.00
95	$30.00-35.00
96	$3.00-4.00
97	$3.00-4.00
98	$15.00-20.00
99	$12.00-15.00
100	$1.00-3.00
101	$45.00-65.00
102	(w/2 pieces of luggage) $55.00-65.00

Photo Number	Price
103	$1.00-3.00
104	$1.00-3.00
105	$35.00-40.00
106	$10.00-12.00
107	$10.00-12.00
108	$4.00-5.00
109	$65.00-85.00
110	$5.00-6.00
111	$20.00-25.00
112	S.A.
113	$6.00-8.00
114	set $5.00-7.50
115	$25.00-35.00
116	w/4 figures $40.00-55.00
117	$6.00-8.00
118	$15.00-17.50
119	$15.00-17.50
120	$6.00-8.00
121	$3.00-5.00
122	$12.50-15.00
123	$24.00-28.00
124	$10.00-12.50
125	$8.00-10.00
126	$6.00-8.00
127	$7.50-10.00
128	$12.00-15.00
129	$2.00-3.00
130A & 130B, with this shape paddle base	$25.00-30.00
131	$1.00-1.50
132	$2.00-3.00
133	$5.00-7.00
134	$2.00-3.00
135	$1.00-1.50
136	$1.50-2.00
137	$3.00-4.00
138	$2.00-3.00
139	S.A.
140	$1.00
141	$1.00
142	$1.00
143	$1.00-1.25
144	S.A.
145	$65.00-80.00
146	$15.00-20.00
147	$6.00-8.00
148	S.A.
149	$45.00-55.00
150	$10.00-12.00
151	$2.00-4.00
152	$2.00-4.00
153	$65.00-80.00
154	$1.50-2.00
155	#460 $5.00-6.00
	All other seals.......$3.00-4.00
156	$1.00-2.00
157	$10.00-12.00
158	$10.00-12.00
159	S.A.
160	$25.00-30.00
161	$65.00-85.00
162	$6.00-10.00

Photo Number	Price	Photo Number	Price	Photo Number	Price
163	$60.00-80.00	232	$8.00-10.00	296	$3.00-4.00
164	$8.00-10.00	233	$25.00-30.00	297	complete $5.00-10.00
165	$40.00-45.00	234	$30.00-35.00	298	$1.00
166	$3.00-5.00	235	$6.00-8.00	299	$3.00-4.00
167	$5.00-7.50	236	$3.00	300	$12.00-15.00
168	$5.00-7.50	237	$8.00-10.00	301	$3.00-4.00
169	$5.00-7.50	238	$4.00-6.00	302	$1.00
170	$8.00-12.00	239	S.A.	303	S.A.
171	$8.00-12.00	240	$5.00	304	$1.00
172	$1.00	241	$8.00-10.00	305	$1.00
173	$1.00-2.00	242	(add $10.00 for cardboard fish) $12.00-15.00	306	$1.25
174	$.50-1.00			307	$85.00-100.00
175	$6.00-8.00	243	$20.00-25.00	308	complete $15.00-20.00
176	$2.00-2.75	244	$50.00-60.00	309AX & 309BX	Gilbert Ad
177	$8.00-10.00	245 Rubber connectors	$25.00-30.00	310	mint $40.00-45.00
178	$15.00-20.00	Steel connectors	$15.00-18.00	311	mint $50.00-65.00
179	$12.00-15.00	246	$4.00-5.00	312	$30.00-35.00
180	$12.00-15.00	247	S.A.	313	$25.00-30.00
181	$1.00-2.00	248	$5.00-6.00	314	complete $25.00-30.00
182	$1.00-2.00	249	$28.00-35.00	315	$8.00-12.00
183	$4.00-6.00	250A, 250B, and 250C	complete $80.00-120.00	316X This version	$15.00-20.00
184	$6.00-8.00			317	$20.00-28.00
185	$5.00-7.00	251A, 251B and 251C	complete $40.00-50.00	318	complete $45.00-50.00
186	$2.00-3.00	252	$8.00-10.00	319	$30.00-35.00
187	S.A.	253	$15.00-20.00	320	$40.00-45.00
188	$1.00-2.00	254	$6.00-8.00	321	$35.00-40.00
189	$12.50-15.00	255	S.A.	322	$40.00-45.00
190	$12.50-15.00	256	complete $8.00-10.00	323	$45.00-50.00
191	$12.50-15.00	257	complete $8.00-10.00	324	$25.00-30.00
192A & 192B	$2.50-3.50	258	complete $4.00-6.00	325	mint $35.00-40.00
193	$12.50-15.00	259	complete $8.00-10.00	326X Gong Bell Ad	
194	complete $12.50-15.00	260	complete $8.00-10.00	327	$8.00-10.00
195	$20.00-25.00	261	complete $20.00-25.00	328X American Logs	$6.00-8.00
196	$10.00-12.00	262	complete $45.00-50.00	Alphabet Blocks	$20.00-25.00
197	$7.00-10.00	263	complete $6.00-8.00	Cart w/Blocks	$20.00-25.00
198	S.A.	264	complete $15.00-18.00	American Plastic Bricks	$8.00-12.00
199	S.A.	265	S.A.		
200	$12.50-15.00	266	complete $20.00-25.00	329	$6.00-8.00
201	$12.50-15.00	267	complete $25.00-35.00	330	$2.00-3.00
202	$20.00-25.00	268	each $2.00	331	$5.00-7.00
203	$5.00-6.00	269	complete $8.00-10.00	332	$12.00-15.00
204	$12.50-15.00	270	complete $12.00-15.00	333	$6.00-8.00
205	$30.00-40.00	271	complete $15.00-18.00	334A & 334B	$8.00-10.00
206	$15.00-20.00	272	complete $8.00-10.00	335	$2.00
207	$5.00-6.00	273	$8.00-10.00	336	$12.00-15.00
208	$2.00-3.00	274	complete $10.00-12.50	337	$3.00-4.00
209	S.A.	275	complete $15.00-20.00	338A & 338B	$12.00-15.00
210	$12.50-15.00	276	complete $8.00-10.00	339	$5.00-6.00
with plastic knob	$8.00-10.00	277	complete $30.00-35.00	340	$3.00-4.00
211	$5.00-6.00	278	complete $20.00-25.00	341	$2.00-3.00
212	each $1.00	279	complete $15.00-18.00	342	$12.00-15.00
213	$15.00-20.00	280 (smaller set S.A.) complete	$15.00-18.00	343	$2.00-3.00
214	$35.00-40.00			344	$3.00-4.00
215	$25.00-35.00	281 complete (classic edition available 1987)	$55.00-60.00	345 & 346	$8.00-12.00
216	$2.00-3.00			347	$6.00-8.00
217	$12.50-15.00	282 complete	$20.00-25.00	348	$15.00-20.00
218	$12.50-15.00	283	$5.00-6.00	349	$10.00-12.00
219	$2.00-3.00	284 complete	$20.00-25.00	350A & 350B	$15.00-20.00
220	$12.50-15.00	285A & 285B complete	$25.00-30.00	351	$20.00-25.00
221 w/2 milk bottles	$65.00-85.00	286	$15.00-18.00	352	$10.00-15.00
222	$1.00-2.00	287	$2.00-3.00	353	$8.00-10.00
223	$25.00-30.00	288	$20.00-25.00	354	$40.00-55.00
224	$25.00-30.00	289	$6.00-8.00	355	$45.00-60.00
225A & 225B	$35.00-40.00	290	$4.00-5.00	356	$45.00-60.00
226	S.A.	291	each $2.00	357	$200.00-250.00
227	$55.00-75.00	292	$15.00-20.00	358	$7.50-10.00
228	$15.00-20.00	293	each $90.00-110.00	359	$7.50-10.00
229	$35.00-40.00	294	$2.00-3.00	360	$6.00-8.00
230	$2.00	295	$6.00-7.00	361	$7.50-10.00
231	$6.00-8.00			362	$3.00-4.00

Photo Number		Price	Photo Number		Price	Photo Number		Price
363		$15.00-20.00	430		$25.00-30.00	494		$20.00-25.00
364	MIB	$35.00-40.00	431	MIB	$75.00-125.00	495		$15.00-20.00
365		$85.00-130.00	432		$50.00-70.00	496	complete	$35.00-45.00
366	MIB	$15.00-20.00	433		$60.00-80.00	497		$5.00-6.00
367	complete	$50.00-75.00	434	complete	$60.00-75.00	498		$110.00-150.00
368		$10.00-12.00	435		$100.00-125.00	499		$75.00-100.00
369A & 369B		$10.00-12.00	436	MIB (orig. box)	$35.00-40.00	500		$15.00-20.00
370		$15.00-20.00	437		$25.00-30.00	501		$35.00-40.00
371		$2.00-3.00	438		$18.00-22.00	502A & 502B		$40.00-50.00
372		$12.00-15.00	439		$15.00-20.00	503A - 503E	MIB	$100.00-150.00
373		$4.00-6.00	440		$15.00-20.00	504A - 504F	MIB	$150.00-200.00
374		$30.00-35.00	441		$6.00-8.00	505	MIB	$110.00-150.00
375	each	$2.00-3.00	442		$30.00-35.00	506		$25.00-35.00
376	set of four	$12.00-15.00	443		$20.00-25.00	507		Rare
377		$6.00-8.00	444		$55.00-75.00	508A & 508B		Rare
378		$100.00-125.00	445	MIB (orig. box)	$18.00-25.00	509		Rare
379		$10.00-12.00	446		$8.00-10.00	510A & 510B		Rare
380		$1.00-2.00	447		$8.00-10.00	511A & 511B		Rare
381		$6.00-8.00	448		$6.00-8.00	512A & 512B		Rare
382	complete	$8.00-10.00	449A & 449B		$1.00-1.50	513		$20.00-25.00
383		$10.00-12.00	450		$15.00-20.00	514	each	$10.00-12.00
384		$4.00-6.00	451		$7.00-10.00	515	MIB	$20.00-22.00
385		$6.00-8.00	452		$20.00-25.00	516		$30.00-40.00
386		$8.00-10.00	453		$25.00-30.00	517	each	$10.00-12.00
387		$12.00-15.00	454		$25.00-30.00.	518		$120.00-145.00
388		$6.00-8.00	455		$100.00-125.00	519	complete	$30.00-35.00
389		$12.00-15.00	456X	T.I.E. Fighter	$15.00-20.00	520		$12.00-15.00
390		$3.00-4.00		Millenium Falcon	$25.00-35.00	521		$12.00-15.00
391A & 391B		$10.00-12.00		Star Destroyer	$25.00-35.00	522		$8.00-10.00
392		$8.00-10.00		T.I.E. Bomber	$50.00-75.00	523		$10.00-12.00
393		$6.00-8.00		Y-Wing Fighter	$20.00-35.00	524		$12.00-15.00
394		$20.00-25.00		Snow Speeder	$20.00-30.00	525		$10.00-12.00
395		$1.00-2.00		Slave I	$20.00-30.00	526		$10.00-12.00
396		$1.00	457		$15.00-20.00	527		$12.00-15.00
397		$2.00-3.00	458		$15.00-20.00	528		$4.00-5.00
398		$2.00-3.00	459		$30.00-40.00	529		$12.00-15.00
399	"Star Wars" logo	$5.00-7.00	460		$8.00-10.00	530		$4.00-5.00
	all others	$1.00-3.00	461	complete	$85.00-125.00	531		$6.00-8.00
400A & 400B	"Star Wars" logo		462		$12.00-15.00	532		$4.00-5.00
	MIP each $5.00-6.00;		463	each	$1.00-2.00	533	set	$55.00-65.00
	all others $2.00-3.00 MIP		464	each	$1.00-2.00	534		$35.00-45.00
401		$25.00-30.00	465	set	$10.00-12.00	535	complete	$40.00-45.00
402		$60.00-80.00	466		$2.00-3.00	536A & 536B		$2.00-3.00
403		$50.00-75.00	467	each	$2.00-3.00	537		$2.00-3.00
404	$60.00-80.00; MIB	$90.00-110.00	468		$2.00-3.00	538		S.A.
405	$50.00-75.00; MIB	$80.00-100.00	469		$4.00-5.00	539		$8.00-10.00
406A & 406B		$25.00-40.00	470		$20.00-25.00	540		$1.50-3.00
407		$6.00-8.00	471		$5.00-6.00	541		$6.50-8.50
408		$35.00-45.00	472		$1.00-2.00	542		$8.00-10.00
409	Original, MIB	$25.00-40.00	473		$10.00-12.00	543		$8.00-10.00
410		$20.00-25.00	474		$1.00-2.00	544A & 544B		$8.00-12.00
411	Original, MIB	$25.00-35.00	475		$2.00-3.00	545		$2.00-3.00
412		$15.00-20.00	476		$2.00-3.00	546		$1.00
413		$25.00-35.00	477		$25.00-28.00	547		$8.00-10.00
414		$15.00-20.00	478		$5.00-6.00	548		$3.00-4.00
415		$15.00-25.00	479		$10.00-12.00	549		$4.00-6.00
416		$25.00-50.00	480		$8.00-10.00	550		$1.00-2.00
417		$45.00-60.00	481		$6.00-8.00	551		$8.00-12.00
418		$12.00-15.00	482		$35.00-40.00	552		$35.00-40.00
419		$12.00-15.00	483		$115.00-130.00	553		$20.00-35.00
420		$12.00-15.00	484		$110.00-125.00	554		$40.00-45.00
421	each	$20.00-25.00	485		$55.00-75.00	555		$375.00-450.00
422		$8.00-10.00	486		$35.00-40.00	556		$175.00-225.00
423		$5.00-7.00	487	complete	$50.00-60.00	557	set	$8.00-10.00
424		$5.00-7.00	488A & 488B		$10.00-12.00	558X	Walking Dog	$30.00-35.00
425		$5.00-7.00	489		$5.00-6.00	559X	Walking Duck	$35.00-40.00
426		$10.00-20.00	490		$8.00-10.00	560X	Dump Truck	$25.00-30.00
427A & 427B		$1.00-1.50	491	complete	$20.00-30.00		Tractor	$35.00-40.00
428		$10.00-12.00	492		$20.00-25.00			
429		$25.00-30.00	493		$10.00-12.00			

Photo Number		Price
561X	Woodie Train	$15.00-18.00
	Oil Truck	$20.00-25.00
	Ice Truck	$20.00-25.00
562X	#754 Train	$25.00-30.00
	Flyer	$25.00-35.00
563X	Clock	$35.00-45.00
	Rolly Ducky	$18.00-22.00
564	complete	$25.00-30.00
565		$25.00-30.00
566		$25.00-30.00
567	In orig. condition	$30.00-35.00
568		$20.00-28.00
569	complete	$18.00-20.00
570		$25.00-35.00
571		$6.00-8.00
572		$12.00-18.00
573		$25.00-30.00
574		$22.00-28.00
575		$22.00-28.00
576		$8.00-12.00
577		$8.00-10.00
578	Barn only	$15.00-18.00
579A & 579B	complete	$20.00-30.00
580	complete	$20.00-25.00
581		$2.00-4.00
582		$3.00-4.00
583		$5.00-7.00
584		$3.00-4.00
585		$2.00-3.00
586		$2.00-3.00
587	(Newer version S.A.)	$2.00-3.00
588	set	$60.00-75.00
589	17 pc. set	$40.00-55.00
590	15 pc. set	$20.00-35.00
591	9 pc. set	$15.00-20.00
592	31 pc. set	$45.00-60.00
593	7 pc. set	$10.00-15.00
	9 pc. set	$15.00-20.00
594	14 pc. set	$20.00-28.00
595	8 pc. set	$12.00-16.00
596	20 pc. set	$25.00-30.00
597	31 pc. set	$30.00-40.00
598	9 pc. set	$20.00-30.00
599		$25.00-30.00
600		$1.00
601		$6.00-8.00
602X	Magazine ad	
603		$25.00-35.00
604		$15.00-25.00
605		$18.00-20.00
606		$12.50-18.00
607		$10.00-12.00
608		$6.00-8.00
609		$5.00-6.00
610		$10.00-12.50
611		$6.00-8.00
612		$6.00-8.00
613		$8.00-10.00
614		$12.00-15.00
615		$8.00-10.00
616		$10.00-12.50
617	complete	$15.00-20.00
618		$15.00-18.00
619		$10.00-12.00
620		$2.00-4.00
621		$2.00-3.00
622		$5.00-7.00
623		$.50-1.00
624A & 624B		$12.00-15.00
625		$4.00-6.00

Photo Number		Price
626	complete	$8.00-10.00
627		$2.00-3.00.
628	each	$2.00-4.00
629		$1.00-2.00
630		$3.00-5.00
631		$2.00-3.00
632		$2.00-3.00
633	set	$8.00-10.00
634	each	$3.00-4.00
635		$3.00-4.00
636		$12.00-15.00
637		$20.00-25.00
638		$6.00-8.00
639		$1.00-2.00
640		$3.00-4.00
641	MIB	$12.00-15.00
642		$12.50-18.00
643		$8.00-10.00
644A		$15.00-20.00
644B		$20.00-25.00
644C		$25.00-30.00
645		$2.00-3.00
646		$2.00-3.00
647		$3.00-5.00
648A & 648B		$2.00-3.00
649		$1.00-2.00
650		$5.00-6.00
651		$3.00-4.00
652		$.50-1.00
653		$1.00-2.00
654		$.50-1.00
655		$.50-1.00
656		$8.00-10.00
657		$3.00-4.00
658		$7.00-10.00
659		$1.00-2.00
660		$12.00-15.00
661		$18.00-20.00
662		$15.00-18.00
663	Pup On Barrel	$3.00-5.00
	Lassie	$8.00-10.00
	Hobo	$15.00-18.00
664XA & 664XB	Magazine ad	
665X	Magazine ad	
666A - 666C		$50.00-75.00
667		$3.00-4.00
668		$8.00-10.00
669		$15.00-20.00
670		$2.00-3.00
671		$35.00-38.00
672	Complete toy	$18.00-22.00
673X	Magazine ad	
674		$10.00-12.00
675		$2.00-3.00
676		$4.00-6.00
677	each	$1.00
678		$2.00-3.00
679		$8.00-10.00
680A - 680C	complete	$5.00-8.00
681	each	$1.00-2.00
682		$20.00-22.00
683		$12.00-15.00
684		$35.00-40.00
685		$35.00-40.00
686		$20.00-25.00
687		$6.00-8.00
688		$6.00-8.00
689		$15.00-18.00
690		S.A.
691		S.A.

Photo Number		Price
692X	Magazine ad	
693		$60.00-75.00
694		$35.00-40.00
695		$6.00-8.00
696	each	$2.00-3.00
697		$2.00-3.00
698		$10.00-20.00
699		$25.00-30.00
700	complete	$95.00-120.00
701		$6.00-8.00
702		$35.00-40.00
703		$2.00-3.00
704		$8.00-12.00
705	complete	$65.00-85.00
706		$25.00-35.00
707		$12.00-15.00
708		$6.00-8.00
709		$4.00-6.00
710		$4.00-6.00
711		$25.00-30.00
712		$6.00-8.00
713		$2.00-3.00
714		$15.00-22.00
715		$18.00-22.00

Prices given on the following group of toys are, in some cases, the result of comparing them to similar toys about which more information is known.

Photo Number		Price
716	set	$35.00-40.00
717	set in box	$45.00-60.00
718		$5.00-8.00
719		$4.00-6.00
720		$30.00-45.00
721	Box	$15.00-20.00
	Dog	$10.00-$12.00
722		$25.00-35.00
723		$35.00-40.00
724		$5.00-6.00
725	as shown	$2.00-3.00
726		$15.00-18.00
727	each	$8.00
728	as shown	$3.00-4.00
729		$15.00-20.00
730	as shown	$5.00-6.00
731		$6.00-8.00
732	as shown	$8.00-10.00
733	There are many variations of these small irons. Prices range from $35.00-$125.00	
734	as shown	$2.00-3.00
735	According to Helene Guarnaccia, this clown belongs to a French ring toss game. No value assigned.	
736		$12.50-15.00
737	Magazine ad	$4.00-6.00

Schroeder's Antiques Price Guide

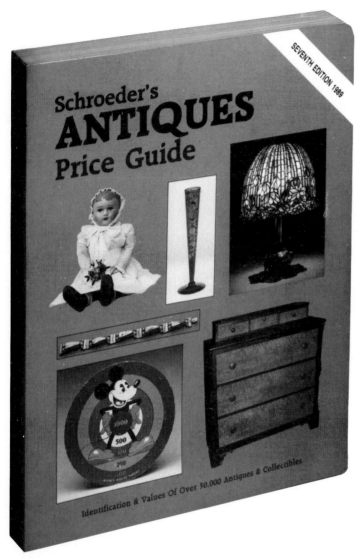

Schroeder's Antiques Price Guide has climbed its way to the top in a field already supplied with several well-established publications! The word is out, *Schroeder's Price Guide* is the best buy at any price. Over 500 categories are covered, with more than 50,000 listings. But it's not volume alone that makes Schroeder's the unique guide it is recognized to be. From ABC Plates to Zsolnay, if it merits the interest of today's collector, you'll find it in Schroeder's. Each subject is represented with histories and background information. In addition, hundreds of sharp original photos are used each year to illustrate not only the rare and the unusual, but the everyday "fun-type" collectibles as well -- not postage stamp pictures, but large close-up shots that show important details clearly.

Each edition is completely re-typeset from all new sources. We have not and will not simply change prices in each new edition. All new copy and all new illustrations make Schroeder's THE price guide on antiques and collectibles.

The writing and researching team behind this giant is proportionately large. It is backed by a staff of more than seventy of Collector Books' finest authors, as well as a board of advisors made up of well-known antique authorities and the country's top dealers, all specialists in their fields. Accuracy is their primary aim. Prices are gathered over the entire year previous to publication, from ads and personal contacts. Then each category is thoroughly checked to spot inconsistencies, listings that may not be entirely reflective of actual market dealings, and lines too vague to be of merit. Only the best of the lot remains for publication. You'll find *Schroeder's Antiques Price Guide* the one to buy for factual information and quality.

No dealer, collector or investor can afford not to own this book. It is available from your favorite bookseller or antiques dealer at the low price of $12.95. If you are unable to find this price guide in your area, it's available from Collector Books, P. O. Box 3009, Paducah, KY 42001 at $12.95 plus $2.00 for postage and handling.

8½ x 11, 608 Pages

$12.95

COLLECTOR BOOKS

A Division of Schroeder Publishing Co., Inc.

Other Books for Toy and Doll Lovers

Character Toys and Collectibles--David Longest	$19.95
Character Toys and Collectibles, Second Series--David Longest	$19.95
Collecting Toys--Richard O'Brien	$14.95
Antique & Collectible Marbles, Second Edition--Everett Grist	$9.95
Children's Glass Dishes, China, and Furniture--Doris Lechler	$19.95
Teddy Bears & Steiff Animals--Margaret Mandel	$9.95
Teddy Bears & Steiff Animals, Second Series--Margaret Mandel	$19.95
The Collector's Encyclopedia of Barbie Dolls--Sibyl DeWein & Joan Ashabraner	$19.95
World of Barbie Dolls--Susan Manos	$9.95
A Collector's Guide to Paper Dolls--Mary Young	$9.95
The Collector's Encyclopedia of Half Dolls--Frieda Marion & Norma Werner	$29.95
Madame Alexander Collector's Dolls--Patricia Smith	$19.95
Madame Alexander Collector's Dolls II--Patricia Smith	$19.95
Madame Alexander Dolls Price Guide #13--Patricia Smith	$4.95
Madame Alexander Ladies of Fashion--Marjorie Uhl	$19.95
Modern Collector's Dolls I--Patricia Smith	$17.95
Modern Collector's Dolls II--Patricia Smith	$17.95
Modern Collector's Dolls III--Patricia Smith	$17.95
Modern Collector's Dolls IV--Patricia Smith	$17.95
Modern Collector's Dolls V--Patricia Smith	$19.95
Patricia Smith's Doll Values--Patricia Smith	$8.95
Patricia Smith's Doll Values II--Patricia Smith	$9.95
Patricia Smith's Doll Values III--Patricia Smith	$9.95
Patricia Smith's Doll Values IV--Patricia Smith	$9.95
Patricia Smith's Doll Values V--Patricia Smith	$9.95
Black Dolls, Identification & Value Guide--Patikii Gibbs	$14.95
The Wonder of Barbie--Paris and Susan Manos	$9.95
World of Barbie Dolls--Paris and Susan Manos	$9.95
German Dolls--Patricia Smith	$9.95
Horsman Dolls--Patikii Gibbs	$19.95
Liddle Kiddle Dolls & Accessories--Tamela Storm-Debra Van Dyke	$9.95
Vogue, Ginny Dolls--Patricia Smith	$19.95
World of Alexander Kins--Patricia Smith	$19.95
French Dolls, 3rd Series--Patricia Smith	$14.95
Stern's Guide to Disney Collectibles--Mike Stern	$14.95
Straight From The Heart: American Rag Doll--Estelle Patino	$14.95

Ask for these popular titles at your favorite bookstore or order direct. Please add $1.00 for postage and handling.

Collector Books ● P.O. Box 3009 ● Paducah, Kentucky 42001